MY NAME IS NOT SIBONGILE
One Woman's Fight For Identity

Bongi Wenyika, PhD

urbanpress

My Name Is Not Sibongile
by Bongi Wenyika, PhD
Copyright © 2019 Bongi Wenyika

ISBN # 978-1-63360-118-5

For Worldwide Distribution Printed in the U.S.A.

Urban Press
P. O. Box 8881
Pittsburgh, PA 15221-0881 USA
412.646.2780

www.urbanpress.us

DEDICATION

I am grateful to dedicate this book to Reggies,
my husband and Thembi, my daughter.
Your support during these past couple of years on
my journey to re-discovery has been a blessing.

To Kudzai, my "Favorite Son." You have
taught me about what life means and you are
the epitome of God's faithfulness. Thank you!

INTRODUCTION

"All my life I had to fight…" is the beginning of a monologue from Oprah Winfrey's character in the movie, The Color Purple, based on Alice Walker's famed novel. Closely related to that statement is an old saying that "anything worthwhile is worth fighting for." While I have found both those statements to be true in my own life experience, they hardly capture the intensity of the battle I have been in since before I can remember. In recent years, I have learned that while I am in the ring fighting for my life and identity, sayings like the two I quoted hardly capture the reality or the scope of the pain and difficulty as I fight.

For the past few years and especially since I entered my forties, I have been in an intense, exhausting battle to discover my purpose—and at times for my very identity as a woman and human being. Throughout my life, I have had to battle through many obstacles, both physical and spiritual, to succeed and achieve what God was leading me to do. In the last few years, as I renewed my efforts to discover purpose and meaning, all hell broke loose in my life. This book will tell you about some of that hell as well as the battles early in life when I was raised by my uncles, having never met my father.

Philippians 1:6 says, "Being confident of this, that he who began a good work in you will carry it on to completion until the day of Christ Jesus." As challenging as it is to hold on to God's promises in His word when the enemy is whispering lies in my ear, I find that looking back at God's past faithfulness helps me keep things in perspective. Focusing on the victories God has brought me through and trusting Him for my future, as chaotic and stressful as it might seem at that moment, has helped me maintain perspective as I fight for my life and purpose. I am confident that He will finish the work He has begun in me.

God has indeed been faithful to me and my family. In this book, I will tell you exactly how. I was born to a single mother and never met my father. I was raised by my extended family in a strict Seventh Day Adventist home. When I was old enough, I rebelled. You may think, "Well, that's natural. All teenagers rebel," and that may be true, but my rebellion was major and cataclysmic. I had an affair with a married man, which created all kinds of complications and suffering for all parties involved.

When that ended, I contemplated ending my life, but went to church where I eventually met my husband. He was (and is) a pastor, so I went from rebel to pastor's wife. We had a child soon after we were married and then a few years later, we were off to the States to fulfill our educational dreams. While in the States, I gave birth to Kudzai, the son who is on the autism spectrum. When I say God is faithful, I have firsthand knowledge about what I speak and write.

I know that my fight for purpose will require the Holy Spirit leading me to the discovery of what it is, but just as important, I need to be present, willing, and available to fight the good fight as the Apostle Paul called it. God created me for a unique purpose, and I owe it to myself and to others to fight for it and fulfill it, whatever it takes.

We should all want to live out our purpose, but many times I have allowed life circumstances to determine what I was doing and then got comfortable in a rut. I let life get in the way instead of seeking what God wants me to do, which will ultimately be fulfilling and rewarding to me and others.

In this book, I want to emphasize to all, but especially women, how important it is to have our own identity. We need to be confident in who we are, and not take our identify from who we marry or who our kids are or what they do (or don't do). That identity cannot be from our tribe but should be personal and meaningful to each of us as individuals—like our fingerprints.

For the first time in my life, I understand how I ended up where I am today. If I hadn't written this book, I would have never thought about some of the life and the things that have happened to me that contributed to where I am and how I think. Having taken time to reflect, however, I can see the reasons I ended up where I was and now face the challenge of having to think and act differently. This book has helped me do that as well.

I haven't figured out my purpose yet, but I've had a glimpse. I don't have all the answers because my journey is different than yours. There are some guideposts along the way, but they are few and far between and I have had to decide which roads to take—and then backtrack when they led in the wrong direction. It's a miracle I'm still here to tell the story but it shows God's faithfulness even when I didn't see it or deserve it. I may have made some wrong turns and landed on some dead ends, but God has seen me through.

I had no father to affirm me. Most of my family did not believe I would amount to much. Thus, I never applied myself, but it turned out I was more prone to academic success than anyone realized. I would not have found that out had we not taken the step of faith to come to the U.S. to further our education. I would be back in Zimbabwe with five or six kids and not be married, based on where I see my mind and life experiences were taking me.

I studied journalism back home and I was good at it, but I probably would be miserable today because I don't think that role would have been fulfilling for me in the long run. The thread that goes through my life as a Christian is God's faithfulness. He has blessed me more than I could have ever imagined. Even though there are still challenges and I must always remind myself that even through the challenges, He is still there and faithful to me.

My Name Is Not Sibongile is a story of redemption and a testimony to the power of the cross and faith. These can be buzzwords in the Christian community and some people can preach a three-point sermon on redemption, the power of faith, and God bringing them through. I have lived that sermon and now want to deliver it to you. As you read the story of my fight for identity and purpose, I pray you will be encouraged in your own battle to find and express who you are.

Sibonginkosi "Bongi" Wenyika, PhD
Ottawa, Kansas USA
September 2019

Chapter 1

A Breakdown

Before I tell you my story of how I got to here, let me tell you where I am—or at least where I was a few years ago. I entered the summer of 2016 with great optimism and expectation. I knew the best of my life was ahead of me and I was on a path that would help me reclaim my life, rediscover who I am, and reengage my career. God opened doors and opportunities for me to better understand myself and reminded me of the many times He had sustained me through His faithfulness. As the summer progressed, I was bothered by the fact that I still had not identified my purpose in life, so I renewed the quest to determine what His purpose for me was beyond being a mother and wife.

As our daughter prepared to return to her university campus for her junior year, we were getting our son ready for his sophomore year in high school. Throughout the summer, his teacher and I worked together to support him so he could have a reasonably good start to a new school year. One of the changes our family made a week before school was to adopt a three-legged dog named Brian O'Malley. He is a mixed-breed rescue service dog that had worked with our son the previous school year. Having him join our family was one of the highlights of the summer. Even though we never imagined having a dog, Brian (or Bri-Bri as I call him) has been a great fit for our family, especially for our son.

During this summer season, my husband was dealing with a stressful situation at work. Despite these potential stressors (dog, new school, special-needs son, hubby's job), I remained optimistic and prayed for peace through what I knew was an approaching but hopefully temporary storm. As the summer progressed and school was just around the corner, my husband's stress level sky-rocketed. During my morning devotions, I was reading the minor prophets and journaling what the Holy Spirit was showing me concerning my purpose. I was still on track, but the storm clouds were all around with light-ning, thunder and tornado warnings were sprinkled in for good measure—and living in the Midwest I have learned how violent those storms can be.

My son's first day of school was the same day my

daughter moved back into the dorms. I was excited to have the whole house to myself for some peace and quiet after a busy and tiring summer. Our son seemed excited about school, especially because Brian was going to school with him. On that first day, I took a nap, relaxed, and journaled some of my thoughts on my social justice interests before it was time to pick him up. While waiting to pick him up, his teacher texted me to give me a heads up that our son had had a rough day. As soon as I read that text, my heart started racing and I braced for what was to come, which was worse than I thought. Our son had such an aggressive episode that it required the assistance of six adults to put him in the car.

After we got him in, I was holding onto the trunk of my car making sure Brian was safe and secure, but I couldn't catch my breath. My son's teacher, his teacher's assistant, his new principal, and four other school staff were watching me as someone helped me to my driver's seat. I began to cry hysterically and still couldn't breathe. I had challenging anxiety before this, but I had pulled it together and gotten into the car, only then to break down in tears on the drive home. There I was, however, on the first day of school, being comforted in the parking lot by what seemed to be the entire school staff. I managed to catch my breath and drive home with tears streaming down my face. When I got home, I called my husband and continued to weep. Later that day, I acknowledged I had experienced an anxiety attack.

I have learned the importance of occasionally disengaging from social media to focus on my life, despite the challenges. This is not easy, but it has been helpful for my mental health and has protected me from comparing my situation to what appears to be the "normal" lives of others. I choose to be grateful for where I am and wherever the Lord wants to take me next. As Galatians 6:9 reminded me recently, "So let us not grow weary in doing good; for if we don't give up, we will in due time reap the harvest."

On first days of school, both Facebook and Instagram are usually full of posts in which parents share their adorable first-day-of-school posts of gleeful, happy children. In 2015, I had seen those posts on our son's first day of school, and I decided in the future to stay away from social media in 2016. I forgot, however, so while I was wondering how my son's first day was going, I once again saw happy faces of students with new teachers and parents smiling as they dropped off their children, obviously confident their children would have a great day. Seeing those posts contributed to the meltdown I had at my son's school when things went so horribly wrong.

For the next two weeks, all the plans I had of resting, writing, and cleaning my house were derailed by his daily aggressive episodes at school. When he was at school, I was anxious. Then when I picked him up, I was hit, punched, and kicked as I helped the school staff load him into my car. My husband's stress levels continued to increase and to make matters even worse, our son's sleep patterns became erratic. During those two weeks, we didn't have a full night's sleep because, while he had no trouble falling asleep, he found staying asleep to be impossible. We have learned there is a correlation between our son's lack of sleep and increased episodes of aggression. As these challenges inundated my daily life, I realized that my purpose focus had undoubtedly intensified the challenges and my quest to discover my calling was being hijacked.

I am learning the importance of not suffering in

silence. Up till recently, I would have internalized how I was feeling about the challenges I was facing and not shared my struggles, which would have magnified them even further. I can no longer afford to do that. I have learned it is okay to text my best friend, Cari, and a few other trusted friends to vent or share how I'm feeling and not think I am being intrusive. In the summer of 2016. I made an appointment with my doctor to make sure that the physical symptoms I was feeling were due to the increased stress and not serious medical issues. As wives and mothers, we tend to take care of everybody else and don't make self-care a priority, which is a big mistake. As flight attendants say on every flight, "In the event of the plane losing cabin pressure, adults should put their oxygen masks on first; then help others." If we as mothers and wives don't take care of ourselves, what good are we going to be to our families if something happens to us?

I share this story not to complain or garner sympathy. It is to describe the circumstances in my life right now as I seek to find purpose and write this book. I want you to know that I could not stop my life to find myself. I had to find myself in the midst of all life's challenges and detours. I suspect you will have to do the same.

My struggle for purpose did not start in the summer of 2016. It started in my mother's womb. Let's go back there now so I can relate the circumstances around my conception and birth.

Chapter 2

Raised By
My Uncles

I was born in Hyde Park Estates, a semi-rural neighborhood in a city called Bulawayo, Zimbabwe's second largest city. I was born into the Ndebele tribe (the Shona are the larger of the major tribes). My mom, whose name is Deborah, got pregnant when she was taking her teacher training, and I don't know where she met my father. One day, she came home to let the family know she was pregnant. In African culture, the man must come and claim responsibility for the pregnancy. From what I understand, my father didn't want my mother to teach, but wanted her to become his wife. My uncles gave her the choice to either continue her education or marry him—but she could not do both. If she continued her education, they offered to help raise her child. My grandmother offered to care for the child if she chose education, and so she chose to remain in school.

Therefore, I was left with my grandmother, who raised me from my infancy until my mother finished her teacher training. I grew up in a house without indoor plumbing or an indoor bathroom. We walked with wheelbarrows and buckets to get water at a communal water source. The first time I recall my mother being home with me was when she started teaching. She was arrested right after Zimbabwe independence for pro-testing teachers' salaries, which were and still are quite low. All that is my earliest recollection of my mother the teacher.

Beginning of grade five in elementary school, I moved in with my uncle and aunt, who lived across the street from my school. My aunt and uncle were strict and tried to keep us under lock and key, but my cousin and I always found ways to do whatever we were told we shouldn't do. We weren't allowed to see movies, but would leave school, watch a movie, and get home before they got home from work.

As I grew up, no one talked about my biological father. I would sense my family's disapproval when some-one asked questions about who their father was, I would overhear family members saying, "How can that person even want to know about their Dad? That man never did anything for them." If I ever asked about my father, that would be their response. I felt my asking might be interpreted as being ungrateful to my family. In our culture, children didn't question things, unlike in the States where we raise our kids to be self-expressive. We don't have any secrets in the U.S. and talk about almost anything with our children. That was not the case in Zimbabwe.

The only time I heard about my biological father was when I did something wrong and one of my uncles would say that I should go find him, even though we had no idea where he was. As a young adult, whenever I entered a relationship of which my family disapproved, one of my uncles would say I was not worthy of their last name and should go look for my father and take on his last name.

I never met my father. As a young adult, I wondered how life would have been if he was in the picture. When I was doing my undergrad studies, we could enroll for a lifelong learning credit. I decided to do a research paper about the impact on girls raised in homes without their fathers. The more research I did, the more I could look back on my life and understand how some of the choices and decisions I made, especially concerning the relationship I will discuss later, were the result of not having a father in my life. I looked for acceptance in all the wrong places when I decided to leave home and be rebellious.

While doing the research project, I cried for the first time because I related what I was learning to my own experience. When my mother was in the States for her last visit, I asked her if she had any more information about my father than what I heard growing up, but she did not. I always wondered about my genetics, medical histories, and other potential issues and how they relate to me and my family. With rampant HIV and AIDS in Africa, I don't know if my father is even alive. I have often wondered if there is someone out there who looks like me. As I have gotten older, I have a resemblance to my mother, but I will never know what parts of who I am came from my father's side of the family. I have no desire to go find him, for that would probably present me with more problems and questions than solutions.

Not having a father in my culture created scenarios in which I had to fight—for justice, for my identity, for my femininity. Even my names were a source of contention. Let me explain. My grandfather emigrated from the nation of Malawi and settled in Bulawayo, Zimbabwe (then Rhodesia). He didn't want to use Chigaru, his Malawian last name, so instead he used the last name Ndlovu so he could more easily assimilate into Zimbabwean culture. That became the last name for everyone on my grandfather's side until my uncles were older and they reverted back to the name Chigaru. Because my father was not there when I was born, I took my mom's and her brothers' last name of Ndlovu.

After my mom gave birth and went back to school, my aunt and uncle took me to get my birth certificate. I didn't realize until we were filing our citizenship paperwork here in the United States in 2016 that my aunt and uncle are listed as my mother and father on my birth certificate. Back then, whoever was applying for the birth certificate had to be the parent, so my uncle stepped in as my father. Because his wife was present, my aunt was listed as my mother. This uncle was my mother's eldest brother who was next in line as my guardian because my grandfather had died. I never lived with this aunt and uncle, but did live with his younger brother and that brother's wife.

When my uncle and aunt went to get my birth certificate, instead of registering me with my actual given first name of Sibonginkosi, they actually registered me using the first name Sibongile. That was not and is not my name, so later I had to make an adjustment. My family didn't refer to me as Sibongile, it was simply a misregistration on my birth certificate. Therefore, I changed my first and last name before I finished high school from Sibongile Ndlovu to Sibonginkosi Chigaru. I don't know of anyone else who had to contest and struggle for their names like I had to do, and it was a precursor to how my life would unfold.

I was quite close to my grandmother, but I do not recall my mother as very affectionate growing up, although she was a great provider. The first time I gave her a hug was when she came for a visit to the U.S. in 2002 for my son's delivery. I went to the only school in Hyde Park Estates for grades one and two. Then my mother started teaching in a township school and transitioned me there. She wanted to be my teacher, but I didn't want that, so she put me in her friend's class. That was soon after independence in Zimbabwe when formerly whites-only schools were open to everyone. When I was in grade three, she decided to enroll me in one of these schools. That meant she had a two-hour drive to drop me off at an all-girls school, drive back, teach, put me in after-school care, and drive back in the evening to get me. As difficult as this was, it was a price she was willing to pay because she and my grandmother both recognized the importance of an education.

Then in fourth grade, she put me in a boarding school so she wouldn't have to drive back and forth. After that, an uncle bought a house across the street from the school. Since he was so close, he offered for me to live with him so my mother would not have to invest so much time and money getting me to school. That's how I started living with my uncle, who later married my aunt, and how I grew up with my two cousins. I talk often to my male cousin who is my age and lives in Canada, but not so much to my female cousin who lives in Europe. One of my memories while living with my uncle and aunt was whenever I did something wrong, I would be shipped off to my grandmother for discipline. When I started menstruating, my grandmother was notified and she gave me the "becoming a woman" talk and what that maturation meant.

I was young when Zimbabwe gained its independence in 1980, and there were and are two main tribes in my nation: the Shona and Ndebele. The two dominant politicians at the time were Robert Mugabe, who was Shona, and Joshua Nkomo, who was Ndebele. My home was in Bulawayo, Zimbabwe's second largest city, which was where Nkomo had his support base. Robert Mugabe enlisted the North Korean army to train the Zimbabwean army on how to use brutal tactics against his opponents, which led to a tragic period called Gukurahundi, during which the army, comprised of mostly Shona, slaughtered their Ndebele opponents, who the Mugabe government had labeled as dissidents. The army would camp near us because we were in a semi-rural area. We went through a couple of years where on weekends we would all be on lockdown and subject to a curfew.

The back part of my grandmother's home was

near a forest and the soldiers would camp there. We were subjected to many random searches—sometimes in the middle of the night, sometimes during the day. The soldiers would count how many people lived there and how many men were present. These tactics and practices were common during apartheid in South Africa and were used as a way to control the population. Post-independence Robert Mugabe used these same methods to silence dissenters. The army would also erect roadblocks to keep an eye on everyone to ensure they were not stockpiling weapons or engaging in covert activity. Every weekend we would need to have enough soap, food, water, and other essentials because we could not go out and about. When Robert Mugabe's Zanu-PF or Joshua Nkomo's ZAPU held rallies, things would simmer and sometimes boil over. We knew at some point helicopters would drop political leaflets, and for the weekend, sometimes through Tuesday, we would be on lockdown. All that was scary for me as a young child.

I was a good student until I transitioned into the formerly whites–only schools, and then I had problems with reading. My mother got me what they referred to as *Lady Bird* books designed to help my reading, which they did. I was a good student until I got to high school and met boys, and then I got distracted. Then for some reason, my family didn't think I would or could pass my O-levels. Every student had to register for Cambridge exams and then make a list of three preferred schools for A-levels. I was disinterested because my family said they didn't expect much from me, and openly said I probably would not even pass. Therefore, I chose two rural schools as my first two, just to stick it to my family, because those schools were far away and in the rural areas. I also chose my all–girls high school in the city, Townsend High School, as my third and last choice.

I wrote my exams and passed, thus qualifying to go to A-levels. The selection process involved all the headmasters and headmistresses going to Harare, the capital city, to choose their students based on the students' first, second, and third choices. Before my Townsend headmistress went to the selection ceremony, I begged her to choose me. When they called my name at the selection meeting, the headmaster of the rural school I had chosen first, Matopo, said because I had chosen them as my number one, that was where I was going instead of returning to Townsend.

Matopo was a rural school that did not even have any running or hot water, for my form five and that is actually where I went to school, starting when I was 18 years old in April of 1989. My cousin had a twenty-first birthday party on December 31st of that year and I experienced a poisonous snakebite before the party and was unable to go back to school. Thus, during my first term of my final year in A-level, I was in the hospital, recovering from a snake bite. How many people do you know that have had to battle and survive something like that? Let me tell you more about that experience in the next chapter.

Chapter 3

Snakebite

I was bitten in 1989 at my cousin's twenty-first birthday party. My uncle and aunt came by and parked their car by the curb. It was raining, and I was talking to them while the rain fell on another cousin and me. My cousin nudged me to get into the car so we could all talk in there instead of standing in the rain. As I got in, my leg got caught under the car and I felt a sharp pain, but I didn't think much of it at the time.

Throughout that night at the party, I had hot and cold flashes, but still didn't suspect anything. Whenever my leg stiffened up, I danced and it felt better. I noticed later that I had two puncture marks through my nylon stockings. Around 3 AM, I decided to sleep so I could make breakfast for everyone in the morning, which I did. When I got home later that afternoon, I told my family there was something wrong with my leg, thinking it got scratched at the party. They also thought nothing of it so I went to sleep that night but woke up drenched in sweat with my right leg feeling heavy.

When I pulled down the covers, my leg was swollen. It was so painful I couldn't get out of bed and had to scream for my aunt. My aunt rushed me to the hospital and they started the admission process, even though they didn't know what was going on. I was assigned a bed in the general women's ward where the care was primitive. I can still see myself, in excruciating pain, moving from the hospital bed to the bathtub to take a bath. I can also still smell the filth.

The food was awful, and I remember the horrible smelling toast and boiled eggs with smashed shells we had for breakfast. My mother came to visit and I told her I could not stand another day there, even though they still did not know what my problem was. By this time, my leg was huge and I could not put any pressure on it. Finally, a surgeon came to look at me and reported that if they delayed treatment any longer, I would lose my leg because my leg was rotting from the inside out. He proceeded to prep me for surgery as quickly as possible.

If they had waited a couple more hours, it would have affected my knee and they would have had to amputate my leg. I woke up after my operation in a private ward room where I was quite comfortable. I learned the surgeon had scraped all the tissue from my foot right up to just below my knee because it was all rotten.

The treatment plan was to keep me in the hospital to regrow the healthy flesh and tissue in my leg. Then they did a skin graft, taking skin from my right thigh and grafting it to both sides of my leg and foot. I spent three months in the hospital, which was around the time of the first Gulf War in 1991. What I didn't realize until recently was that the bite and hospital care were actually traumatic and left me emotionally scarred. Back then, especially in Africa where mental health is viewed as taboo, or is ignored, I didn't recognize I lived through a traumatic experience, but looking back, I did.

The doctors suspected a puff adder had bitten me. The surgeon later explained that when a puff adder snake bites someone, the venom is localized in the area of the bite. He explained that if it had been any other snake, I would have gone to sleep and never awakened. I would have died. Thank God it was a puff adder because the damage to the leg was contained. It wasn't until years later that doctors concluded the snake bite had resulted in permanent nerve damage to my leg, which limits me physically.

After that, my family had even less confidence in my academic ability because I missed a term in school and they felt there was no way I would pass my A-levels. They wanted me to repeat the year, but I refused. My mother secured remedial tutoring and I passed my A-levels and then decided to go to journalism school. The constant theme among my family was they really didn't think I was going to pass. I was not good in math, but during my undergrad studies here in the States, I got an A in Algebra and called my uncle to say, "See? I can do math if I am motivated enough and have the right teacher."

Growing up in the Seventh Day Adventist church, we weren't allowed to wear trousers, earrings, or makeup. We had a lot of legalism and *don'ts* and not God's grace or a daily personal relationship with Christ. From sunset Friday until sunset Saturday, we were not permitted to do any work around the house and were forbidden to enjoy any entertainment or recreation. We attended City Center Church, which used to be a white church but was mixed when I was growing up. I was part of the youth group and preached my first sermon in a Seventh Day Adventist youth service focused on Luke 8:4–15, which is known as the parable of the sower.

I was quite involved in the church, but I had no choice. The youth group was where and how we socialized as teens. We had to dress a certain way for church and could wear nothing casual. What's more, my aunt and uncle had a child who I helped raise when my aunt went to Canada to do her undergrad studies. I was a teenager by then, and discovered later that they raised him differently than they did my cousins and me. I tease them to this day and tell them that by the time he came along, we had exhausted them or they had mellowed. He now lives in the U.S. and works in New York.

In 1987, when I was 16, my mother married. Her husband was widowed with three children and one of his daughters had a child. Mom moved in with him and his three adult children and his grandchild. One of my stepsisters was just finishing teacher training, and another one had flunked her O-levels and wasn't doing much. I don't think my stepbrother ever graduated high school.

When I was at the house and he was there, everything had to be locked up because he would steal things and was on drugs and drank alcohol, even as my stepfather berated him for it because he was a devout Seventh day Adventist.

My stepfather was from the Xhosa tribe in South Africa, and there was a section outside Bulawayo where most of the Xhosa-speaking people lived. Their culture was very different from ours and they still spoke mostly Xhosa. I would also label some of them as chauvinists. A lot of pride was derived from males and sons as compared to females. My mother immersed herself in their culture. In hindsight, it felt like she neglected some relationships with her family and immersed herself in my stepfather's life and those of his relatives. When the relatives visited the city, they all stayed at their house. So even as a 16-year-old, I was concerned my mother was being taken advantage of. Then as I got older, I understood she wanted to be married, and that could have been her way of getting a family outside of being with my grandmother.

When my stepfather died in 2002, they wanted to come in and take everything out of the house despite all that she had given to his kids and family. My relatives called me in the States to tell me what was going on and what she was going through. It got to the point where I called and tried to convince her to move out of the home, even if it meant she would only have a few shingles over her head. My stepbrother justified what he was doing by saying it was not her house. I felt she should let them take everything, but my mother isn't very good at doing things like that. Who am I to say she was wrong?

When I went back to Zimbabwe in 2016, I found

out she had been actively continuing the development of the property at my stepfather's rural home. Although I don't think this is a great idea, I had to let it go because it wasn't my decision or responsibility and there was nothing I could do about it. I am getting ahead of myself, however, for I must tell the story of what I went through, or should I say the fight I had, to get a university education.

Chapter 4

Fighting For
An Education

As I look back on my early years, I know now that I was in a fight since birth for who I was and who I belonged to. I had no father, my mother was not present while she went to school for my first few years, and I was raised by my grandmother, then my uncle. I went to a few schools but was not seen as a good student and was given little chance for academic success. My church was legalistic and told us more about what we could not do than what we could do.

When I became a teenager, I wasn't supposed to date due to my strict family, but nevertheless I started dating a young man who attended our Seventh Day Adventist Church. He was attending a boarding school, so our dating was mostly through writing letters. I had a small book bag and stored all the letters we wrote back and forth in there. I came home one day and my aunt and the maid had gone through and read all the letters. They thought doing so would curb my behavior, but it was just fanning the flame.

Before that situation, however, the first relationship I had was with my cousin's friend who also attended a boy's boarding school. He befriended my cousin under the guise that we could start dating, which was really talking on the phone, visiting in person, and letter writing. That summer he spent a lot of time at our house and my aunt and uncle thought he was coming to spend time with my cousin. He was from a well-off family so after he went back to school, he was able to call and send cards. Most boys his age would not have been able to do that.

At Christmas time, his family had a party for teenagers and he asked if we could go. My uncle asked, "You mean with those people who drink?", which was another forbidden activity. My cousins and I begged and begged, and finally they dropped us off and said we could spend 90 minutes at the party before they would pick us up. We went to the party and had a great time, feeling like real teenagers because finally they had let us out of the house at night to attend a party.

This boy had bought perfume for my Christmas

present and dropped it off at our house with the maid, thinking she would keep it secret. The maid told my aunt and my family even opened his card. When we got home from being out, we knew something was wrong. We always knew when we were in trouble because during devotions (which we had every night), my uncle would open Proverbs and choose the verses that described how disobedient children were to be disciplined and instructed in the ways of life. My female cousin was always a good girl so she was looking at my male cousin and me, wondering what we had done. When devotions were over, my uncle did all the praying, another sign that something was wrong. We knew that once he said amen, we needed to run for it. As soon as he finished praying, he opened his eyes and sternly told us to sit down. My cousin and I still joke about this almost every time we talk.

My uncle started off by looking at my male cousin and saying, "I don't know how you could let a snake into this house. How could you let that boy come in here and go after one of your sisters?" We didn't yet know the boy had sent the perfume. My uncle swung, but we were expecting it and had backed away while he read us the riot act. They thought that was going to settle the issue, but instead, it made me even more eager to break away from their controlling ways. Throughout high school, I dated on and off.

I always enjoyed writing and English was my favorite class. I would write short stories in high school and as I did, it became apparent to me that I wanted to be a journalist. I could not qualify for university entrance based on the scoring system Zimbabwe used at that time, which was a blessing in disguise. Therefore, journalism school became the next-best option for me. I sat for the exam and the interview, and I did well in those, so I knew it was a good fit for me. To be honest, journalism school subjects came naturally to me because I don't ever remember studying. I was one of the students who sat at the back of the class and always made fun of the professor and fellow classmates who tried to imitate media personalities on television or disc jockeys on the radio. I made some lifelong relationships in journalism school. Thanks to social media, I still keep in touch with some of them.

I attended a two-year program at a polytechnic school in Harare. The program was modeled after the U.S. college-credit system and was designed by a man named Dr. Muzorewa, the son of the first democratically-elected prime minister in Zimbabwe. One of the classes I took was shorthand, but I couldn't stand it and the instructor, so I didn't go to class for two months. It didn't help that the class was at 8 AM. Dr. Muzorewa was my adviser and called me into his office one day to say, "Chigaru, are you aware that if you don't start showing up to your 8 AM shorthand classes, you will never graduate?" I responded, "Dr. Muzorewa, are you aware that I have developed my own shorthand and that I will not only pass, but do very well?" I had developed my own fast way of writing and considered that course and most of the other classes a breeze. Even so, I enjoyed my experience in journalism college.

My first recollection of surrendering to my family's low expectations of my academic performance was when they insisted that unless I repeated Form five, I couldn't pass my A-levels. So at that point I didn't care if I did or not. If I had studied as much as I could have, I would have done much better. After missing a semester of school, I exceeded their expectations. Leaving home and going away to college and getting my freedom only fueled my rebellion. I would party Monday through Friday and go to church on Saturday as a good Adventist, only to go to a party on Saturday night. I would wake up at 11 AM on Sunday and start all over again.

After my mother's marriage, I would visit her on weekends and holidays and stay with her new family and my stepfather's extended family. I thought about my father from time to time, and gradually lost my sense of identity because it didn't seem I belonged anywhere at the time. I couldn't identify with my mother and step-dad and all that was going on with them. I lived with my aunt and uncle while my mother took care of all my school costs and clothing, but I could not identify with my uncle's family either. When I was under his roof, I was always walking on eggshells trying not to offend my female cousin who was upset that her father had divorced her mom. I made every effort to stay in good graces with my aunt who was coming into the family.

It was a balancing act, and I never felt I belonged anywhere. If I ever did anything wrong, I was shipped back to my grandmother for discipline. When I reached puberty, I was shipped to my grandmother to have the talk—not to my mother, but my grandmother. When I emigrated to the States, I was more upset leaving Zimbabwe and my grandmother, knowing most probably I would never see her alive again, than I was leaving my mother. That's how close I was to my grandmother.

When I got involved in my wrong relationship in my rebellious years, all my uncles wanted input and had an opinion—even though I didn't care. I wondered how things would have been different if I had a father. Then I would be accountable to only one person, not a whole committee of people who each had a point of view. At times when I messed up, I was shipped to another uncle, whose wife didn't like me being there, and that was tough. That even made the wrong relationship more attractive because it was an escape.

As if my life wasn't difficult enough, I was about to make decisions that would make my fight for life even more intense and challenging. I look back and wonder what I was thinking, but I wasn't. I was responding to heart issues I did not even know were present, and it almost cost me the very life I was seeking to find.

Chapter 5
Secrets

After graduating from the Mass Communication and Print Journalism Program at the Harare Polytechnic in Zimbabwe, I applied to the Columbia University journalism program and put in applications at several other U.S. schools. From as far back as I can remember, I wanted to earn a journalism degree from an American university. My grandmother, who did not have a fifth-grade education, encouraged me because she understood the value and stressed the importance of education. I wanted to gain an education and create a better life for myself. Growing up in Zimbabwe, we were taught that education was the only way to obtain new opportunities and that the measure of our success and the guarantee of a comfortable life were found in getting an education.

After completing high school, most young women in Zimbabwe went to college. After that, they started working to establish a career and then got married. When I graduated from journalism school, marriage was not a priority because I was in my rebellious phase. I thought if I ever wanted to have children, I could be a mother without necessarily getting married. Clearly this was a season of life when I had walked away from my relationship with God. During college, I had sporadically gone to church, but I did not have a relationship with Christ.

College was interesting because I enjoyed having a cohort of classmates who became close friends. We enjoyed partying, cutting up, and giving our lecturers a hard time. We were the students who sat at the back of the class, made wise cracks during lecturers, and never studied. Although we were financially poor, we had a vibrant life on campus, which included partying, drinking, and smoking. I smoked my first cigarette on a friend's dare, which was ludicrous.

As a twenty-year-old journalism grad, one of my uncles helped me get a job as a paid intern at an internationally-recognized media organization. My life was filled with possibilities I could not have imagined as a child growing up in a humble home that had no running water or indoor plumbing. After writing my final college exams, I needed to check out of the dorms, so one of my uncles called to tell me I would be moving in with him and his wife and that meant I could stay in Harare. I moved in with them and started working. During the first days when I started living with them, I felt like my aunt did not welcome me there. I wondered if my uncle had discussed with her that I would be moving in. It was challenging because I felt like I was an inconvenience and unwelcome. The atmosphere was tense, and I felt unwanted and out of place.

Months later, after a series of events, some partly my fault, I was shipped off to another uncle who was engaged to be married. In a nutshell, this was the story of my life with my uncles. My entire life, I felt my mom deferred decisions concerning me to what felt like a committee of her brothers, and once they reached a consensus, that is what I was expected to do.

As soon as I started the internship, my boss who was another uncle's friend, showed an interest in my work and offered to mentor me. His mentoring involved advice on the profession, editing my work, giving me feedback, taking me with him to presidential press conferences at the State House, and sending me out on assignments and interviews on a variety of issues like the economy, trade, commercial farming, and human-interest stories.

Even though I had interned at a newspaper, corporate magazine, and local news agency while in college, getting the paid internship at this prestigious organization was a big deal. Having a renowned journalist offer to be my mentor was another great opportunity. The work was challenging, but the training I had received kicked in and I was holding my own while also learning a great deal in the process. I started building relationships with co-workers and before long, we were having lunch together.

After long days in the newsroom, most journalists

in the city would meet at a local hotel bar to unwind and talk shop. I went there several times, but once my uncles found out, they put a stop to that. Looking back, it is no wonder I became rebellious. It seems to me that they put a stop to any semblance of freedom I tried to attain. I still don't fully understand what their thinking and motivation were. At that point, I just saw them as buzzkills. Spending time with other journalists was a rite of passage for any young reporter, and I felt robbed of that experience. In hindsight, I also think that not being able to socialize with colleagues after work left me isolated and, in part, teed up for what happened next.

Weeks into my internship, I received results from my journalism exams and I had passed—I was a bona fide journalist. I was excited, and my mentor asked to take me to dinner to celebrate and I agreed. In hindsight, if I had known what was to follow, I would not have accepted that dinner invitation. What started as an innocent dinner to celebrate my success and entry into the profession and field I loved, developed into a scandalous, inappropriate relationship with a married father of three children.

The time in my life when my professional aspirations and dreams were coming true became the beginning of a relationship comprised of secret meetings in bars, hotel rooms, trips out of the country, and weekends away to hide the relationship. Mind you, during the beginning of this affair, I was still living with the aunt and uncle who didn't seem to want me living with them. It was easy to hide the relationship because my aunt never paid much attention to me and my uncle stayed out late nearly every night. Thinking back, I was the perfect candidate to find herself in this situation because I was a child raised without a father and the attention I received from my lover filled a void I didn't know I had.

In the office, I was always looking over my shoulder because I knew I was doing something wrong, but I had the strange ability to detach myself from the situation. One night in a hotel room, the first time I recall feeling pressured and cornered, I told my him to back off and said if he didn't, I would scream rape. Although I did not feel unsafe, I regretted that I had placed myself in that kind of relationship with him. He did back off and we left the hotel. In subsequent months, he alluded to this incident and questioned if I would have screamed out and I assured him I would have.

The relationship continued and months later, I suspected I was pregnant. I was scared out of my mind and took a pregnancy test that proved I was indeed carrying a baby. We never discussed keeping the baby, but he was adamant we couldn't keep the baby. When I think back to who I had become and where I was emotionally, I don't recall feeling anything. In hindsight, I was in survival mode and numb to the reality of being pregnant with this man's child. I was out of my league not only age-wise but also emotionally and was not equipped to handle the situation.

Being 20 years older than I, he had the upper hand and control in the relationship. I have suppressed this part of my past for so long that trying to recall it now has been not only emotionally challenging, but difficult to remember every minute detail. I recall that he made several calls and then told me he had found a medical doctor who would "help us deal" with the pregnancy. He made an appointment with the doctor and we went to the appointment together. He told the doctor I was pregnant and wanted to get an abortion. He asked the doctor, who was his friend, to refer us to an OBGYN who conducted abortions. Thinking back, I wonder if this was the first time he had asked his friend for this type of referral because the doctor did not hesitate to name an OBGYN. Mind you, abortions in Zimbabwe were and are illegal.

When I was a freshman in high school, my best friend from elementary school had an abortion and died. Because abortions are taboo and illegal, I was not allowed to attend her funeral. A year or two after my abortion, I also lost a cousin to a suspected abortion. Although she was older than I, we had grown up together and she was like an older sister to me. I was permitted to attend my cousin's funeral. Even though I had lost a friend to an abortion, I don't remember ever second-guessing my decision to have one. I don't recall ever weighing the risk I was taking, which could have killed me. When I think back, whatever suggestions this older man made, I went along with them. It seems my demeanor and interactions with and toward him were detached, robotic, and void of love or emotion.

We were referred to an OBGYN in the Avenues suburb of Harare and made an appointment. As I later found out, this doctor performed illegal but "safe" abortions in his medical practice for those who were willing and able to pay a hefty price for them. We went together for the initial consultation, but on the day of the abortion, he dropped me off outside the doctor's clinic and picked me up at the end of the procedure.

There I was, sitting in the waiting room, alone and trying not to lock eyes with other women who were probably there for medical issues, while others were pregnant. Eventually, I was escorted to a dark, sterile room, and I could hear my heart beating out of my chest. That is as much as I can recall. All I remember is he picked me up and later dropped me off at my uncle's house where I spent the weekend alone, taking an aggressive cocktail of antibiotics to ensure that I would not develop an infection. I never had a follow up appointment with the OBGYN or any other doctor. We also never talked about the abortion after it happened; somehow life just moved on.

A few months later, he helped me move into an apartment. Soon after, he "left" his family and moved in with me, but within weeks, a co-worker found out about the relationship and tipped off his wife as to where we were living. He was soon fired from his job and convinced me to resign as well, which I did. If I knew then what I know now, I would have filed a sexual harassment charge against him, because he used his position, power, and authority to prey on me, a naïve, younger woman.

His wife called my uncle and told him everything and all hell broke loose. She then came to the apartment and confronted us early one morning and before long, the phone was ringing off the hook from my family. The news of my disgraceful behavior spread quickly as news about me usually did. My business was everybody's business and everyone had an opinion. Being 22 years old at the time, I was in way over my head.

There were brief moments of clarity when I stopped and asked myself, *How did you get yourself in this mess? How did you find yourself in a relationship with someone 20 years your senior, who was married and had three children? How did your life become one secretive decision and rendezvous after another? How did you get here? As a recent college graduate who had my career starting ahead of my peers, how could you have let yourself get to this place?*

Thinking back, this season in my life is a blur, interspersed with sporadic clarity. At this juncture, drinking alcohol and smoking stopped being a fun activity, and was more a way to try and cloud my realization of how wrong my life decisions were and how broken I felt inside. Even though we did not talk about the abortion, having been raised as a believer, deep down I couldn't shake the thought that I had killed a baby and I could not talk to anyone about it. The only person I told about the abortion was my husband before we got married.

When I started this journey of rediscovery, for some reason it did not occur to me that some of the traumatic experiences I have been through, especially having an abortion among a plethora of other experiences, contributed to me losing myself. As I emotionally deal with these past, painful experiences in my life, it's easy to understand how easy it was to lose myself. I had been carrying secrets, shame, guilt, trauma, loss, anger, and inadequacy before God. It is a miracle I have been able to maintain a semblance of healthy functioning. When we first got married, I recall my husband telling me I had serious anger issues. At the time, I didn't understand what he meant, but during this season of rediscovery, I now get it. I now know and am still learning that these life experiences, as devastating as they have been, do not define me. God is using what the devil intended to destroy me for my good. Realizing that and openly talking about my life experience and testimony release me from the hidden secrets and spiritual hang-ups that have held me bound for so long.

I thought my life was over and ruined but little did

I know that I was close to meeting my life partner and that relationship would be the one God would use to get me back on track with Him and with my search for purpose and identity. Let's move on to that part of my life in the next chapter.

Chapter 6

Marriage

When my inappropriate relationship with a married man came to an end and he moved back home to his wife, I was left in the house we had rented, waiting to figure out what my next steps would be. At that point, I was a 22-year-old woman who had given eighteen months of my life to a married man and also been through the traumatic experience of killing a baby. I did not have a job or an income and I could not turn to my family. Needless to say, I was in a difficult and desperate situation, so suicide did cross my mind.

I found a Sunday newspaper and saw an ad promoting Hear the Word Church. I said to myself, *God, if You are as real as I think You are, when I go here I am going to experience something.* That's how I ended up in church that Sunday. It was either harm myself or try this church that I had ridiculed during my party days at college. I had given my life to the Lord in grade five through the Scripture Union ministry, which was a ministry in Zimbabwe's schools. I was involved in church and in the Union throughout high school.

I attended Hear the Word Church because I was desperate for change. No sooner had I taken my seat when the pastor stopped the music and gave an invitation for people to come forward for prayer then and not at the end of the service, which was the norm. I was one of the people who ran up there because I knew I had walked away from the Lord and was desperate to find Him again.

During the same service, the pastor moved in the Spirit, departing from his message and identifying needs people who were present had, once again inviting them forward for prayer. He said there were some who felt pressure to follow through on some decisions they made, even though the Holy Spirit was speaking to them, causing them to wonder if they had chosen the right direction. If that description fit any of us, he invited us to come to the altar and have God speak to us.

At that time, Reggies, who is now my husband, was scheduled to meet and pay a dowry to marry someone else. As it turned out, I was on one side of the altar and Reggies was on the other side of the altar where God spoke to him not to pay the dowry for the young lady who was also present that day in the church. We were able to connect the dots of this story only after we started dating. Reggies obeyed the Lord and broke off the relationship.

Reggies was already established in the church when I got there and was known as a man who befriended everyone. He hosted parties at his house and was the social butterfly of the church. He had a cadre of friends but I had few friends when I joined, and that's why I became part of the young adults group, made up mostly of Reggies' friends.

It became clear right after we started dating that Reggies was an eligible bachelor who was set to marry someone else. I quickly became unpopular because the common perception was that I interrupted those plans—although God was the one who had directed him to break it off with the other woman. When we first met, Reggies was set to resign from his pharmaceutical sales position to go into ministry.

When I joined the church, the eligible single women never liked the fact that women who were new members in the church started dating most of the eligible bachelors. When I joined the young adult's group, it was apparent that people were dating each other, breaking up, and then dating others in the group. Because of my history, I decided not to date for the sake of dating. If I dated someone, I wanted to feel l had the kind of relationship that could potentially lead to marriage. I was done with serial dating without any purpose, or getting into a relationship just to date.

One Sunday night, Reggies' ministry mentor invited us to sit in the front row to fill out the seats. It was obvious by then that we were courting with intentions towards marriage. One of the ushers who was friends with the young lady Reggies had been set to marry became verbally abusive toward me at the end of service. She asked me who I thought I was to come in and grab an eligible bachelor who I knew was going to marry someone else. That gave me a quick introduction not only to ministry, but also life in a church like Hear the Word.

Reggies told me on our first date that he was going to marry me. I laughed at him and told him he was such a jerk. I was thinking, *Who does that?* He was quick to remind me on our wedding night that he told me so, and he reminds me every anniversary saying, "Didn't I tell you?" I respond that he did, but I wouldn't advise any young person to do that. He told me early on in our relationship that ministry was his life and not his vocation. He wasn't going to decide one day to go to medical school or do something different. He felt he was called to the ministry, not part time, but as a career.

I responded that I couldn't say the same but asked for time to fast and pray so I could know if God was calling me to ministry as well. I didn't want to wake up years down the road and discover this wasn't the life for me. I asked him not to call me for two weeks while I prayed and fasted, waiting to hear from God that this was His will for me. Eventually, God revealed that this was His plan for my life and our lives. With the challenges we faced when we moved to the U.S. so Reggies could attend Oral Roberts University, I thank God I had taken the time to fast and pray. If that wasn't what God wanted for me, those tough times would have been even worse.

After we got married, my husband was already an assistant youth pastor and I didn't have a transition period to learn more about what it meant to be a ministry wife. I went from dating a pastor and volunteering with the youth to being expected to fulfill a role that wasn't clearly defined. Based on my personality (more on that later), I need things spelled out for me, but not dictated to me.

To make matters worse, I didn't have a conventional nine-to-five job. At that time, I was working full time as a journalist and would receive an assignment in the morning and then have to call Reggies to inform him that I was going out of town to interview someone. That prevented me from being as involved in the church as I was expected to be—but I had no idea that was what was expected of me. It was confusing to say the least.

I wasn't ready to be a pastor's wife. My Seventh-day Adventist upbringing did not prepare me, and I was also an instant mom after our wedding. We got married in April and our daughter was born in September. I didn't have the history to know how to juggle it all or meet the many expectations being placed on me. What's more, Reggies already knew what his calling was but I didn't—except that I was to be his wife and we were involved in ministry, mostly because he was involved in ministry.

I thought I knew what I was supposed to do and be but I didn't. I was still rebuilding my relationship with the Lord and learning how to be a wife to my husband and mother to my child. I did not have the energy to do it all, and no one took me aside to mentor or train me in the way of life we had chosen—or that was chosen for us. I was back at it trying to find myself.

I soon discovered that I did not understand much about who I was and was not, or what my strengths and gifts were. I had done no internal work to have a life or identity of own. When I finally was able to sit and take a

DISC personality profile, I began to understand more of who I was, which has greatly aided in my search for who Siboginkosi really is.

My personality profile indicates that I am a situational extrovert. Once I get to know someone, I can be open and transparent, but I like to get to know them before I open up. It takes me a while to warm up to someone and to get to know them. That's who I am. My husband is just the opposite; everyone he meets is an immediate friend. Our personality differences showed up in many ways.

I had serious morning sickness with both our babies to the point that before we had our daughter, I was hospitalized when I was three months pregnant. I couldn't keep anything down and had to be given fluids intravenously. I could only eat certain things. The only things that would stay down were things that I craved.

One Friday night right after we got married and I was pregnant, I had a craving for offal. I called Reggies and asked if he could go to a Chinese restaurant down the street and get some for me. He had a youth meeting that night and drove to our apartment to tell me he was not going to get me any offal because he had a commitment to the ministry. He could not be driving around looking for Chinese restaurants just because I was craving offal. We had a huge fight over that. *What do you mean you can't go pick this up for me?* The next day he went and got some for me and all I could keep down was one bite.

Reggies' personality came alive with all the youth and he needed the affirmation of that meeting. What he was doing was who he was. I could not relate to it and wanted him to focus on me and my needs. He needed the crowd and I didn't, and it took me a long time to understand that—and for him to understand why I was not as energized by many relationships like he was. If I have one or two close friends, I am okay. Since moving to the States, I have had two friends who were independent of meeting while working together. One is Lisa who I met in Tulsa and my best friend, Cari. Cari and my friendship is one where we can call each other about anything and we each know the other will be there to listen, with no judgement, but we walk away feeling loved and cared for. We check on each other every week. I miss her because she recently moved from Oklahoma to Florida.

Reggies and my personality differences would manifest any time a church service ended. When it was over, I was thinking, *Okay, we need to go. I have to pick up the baby and go home but I see Reggies is still socializing.* We had a few arguments and he would say, *Can't you just say hello to a few people and then go home?* He was and is a social butterfly, but I wasn't and am not. Sometimes I would just have to suck it up and pretend to be the cordial wife he wanted me to be and his role expected, even if I did not want to be.

When we were assistant youth leaders, there was a hairstylist in Harare who was wildly popular and did a wonderful job cutting my textured hair. I had made an appointment with him to do my hair on a Friday night when we had youth meetings. I left work early to get my hair cut, which was important to me. He was not done with me until around 8 PM.

When I arrived late to the youth meeting, Reggies was upset that I was late for youth, but for me my haircut was important. That was the only appointment I had that was for me, something I wanted or needed to do.

Those personality differences presented a challenge, but my style is to avoid confrontation whenever possible, so I lost myself by trying to do what other personalities wanted or expected from me. Who he was wasn't wrong; it was just him, but the same was true for me.

Those types of things are typical for any young couple, but they became more problematic because we were young, I was young in the Lord, we were in ministry, and I was not sure of who I was. On the other hand, Reggies was quite sure of what he was called to do. He found it easier to relate to these young people, whereas I didn't. I did not think it was my calling at first, but we made it work until we started pastoring adults, which was much easier for me. I could relate to other couples even though people we befriended were generally older than we were.

Before long, I was overshadowed by the expectations of what it meant to be a pastor's wife. I did not choose ministry; I wanted a career, but it was another fight for identity and purpose, one that in some ways I am still waging. The pressures and expectations of church work and ministry were intense. Many wanted to curry favor with the senior pastor's wife and would bend over backwards to do things she wanted the way she liked them done. One of the challenges was *everyone* was positioning themselves to do things she was interested in—except for me. I was not raised in a church with a culture like that, and I didn't have lifelong friends there who could walk me through the cultural and relational expectations.

The church held an annual conference that attracted people from all over the world, and the pastor and his wife expected the other church pastors and wives to entertain those in attendance. During our first conference, I was pregnant and we were staying at the hotel attached to the conference center hosting the meetings. I was sleeping there but going to work every day, and then attending evening services. We were expected, whether it was before or after service, to be there chatting with the guests and members of the congregation. I didn't have the energy or stamina to do that and because I was either unwilling or unable to do so, I felt cut off from social interaction. I never really had any interaction with the pastor and his wife and was concerned it affected Reggies' stature within the church.

If I had known my DISC profile characteristics at that time including my strengths, weaknesses, talents, and leadership skills, I would have been in a better position to navigate to where my passion for ministry was. I would have been a better version of myself than I was at that time. Looking back, I did the bare minimum of what was expected of me. I made our home as functional and comfortable as possible for Reggies so he could perform ministry and continue to work, a pattern that continued for many years.

It was easy for me to lose myself because I didn't know who I really was. Part of that goes back to my childhood of not knowing where I belonged, or having a sense of identity or the confidence to express myself. Looking back, I often coasted through life doing the bare minimum of what those around me expected me to be. It's not surprising that I lost myself in all these different areas and stages of my life. That coupled with being a pastor's wife who is often defined in terms of the ministry partner, caused me to measure up to a shifting standard that was not well-defined.

I learned from my DISC profile that I am someone who likes things clearly spelled out. In my marriage, when we say we are going to do something, my expectation is that it is what we are going to do. When Reggies operates according to his personality, however, that is simply a guideline of what we *may* do. He will switch things in the middle and it used to drive me crazy. I say, *We set out to do something specific, so why are we changing things now?* He replies, *A better way to do something has emerged.* I learned by studying my DISC profile that is who I am, but it also gave me understanding of who he is so I can better equip myself to stand my ground or be flexible, according to the need. I am not so ready now to yield with his flexibility, but when I do, I understand where he is coming from along with the source of my stress.

I do well when given details, and that has come in handy with Kudzai, our child on the autism spectrum. My style was perfect when it came to overseeing his medications—when, how much, and maintaining an adequate supply. On the flip side, I procrastinate, which is interesting to me, because one would think that, since I pay attention to details and am organized, I would not procrastinate—but I do. I have learned some of my procrastination is due to the fact that I am a perfectionist, and I will wait until I have the perfect way figured out before I do something. Also, I am learning that I don't undertake chores unless I know there is a possibility I will complete them.

As a perfectionist, I also took on too much in terms of our family because I thought if I did it myself, it would be done correctly. That caused me to take on more than I should, which has also contributed to my losing myself. The next chapter will describe our journey to the United States, the land of opportunity, where I was about to engage a new front in my war to find myself and fulfill my purpose. My journey was about to get more complicated and complex.

Chapter 7

Coming to America

Right after I finished journalism school, I knew I wanted to come to the U.S. to further my education. I went so far as to send an application to Columbia University because they had a great journalism school. When I met Reggies, I discovered we both wanted to further our education abroad. Reggies applied to get a masters in laboratory science in Germany and had been accepted.

While he was considering whether to go to

Germany, his mentor in the church asked Reggies if he wanted to marry a Zimbabwean or a foreigner. The man was trying to tell Reggies to wait until he met someone local, in Zimbabwe, get married, and then go abroad, making sure his partner also had a desire to go abroad. After we got married, we decided to wait a few years before we moved to the States. Initially, we thought we would move to Pittsburgh, but then we ended up in Tulsa, Oklahoma. We moved in May of 2000, right after we celebrated our fourth wedding anniversary.

It was a tough transition. We had no idea where we were going to live when we got to the States. An American friend had helped shepherd us through the process and the U.S. embassy interview to get our visa application completed and approved. When we came to Tulsa, we had to deal with the U.S. immigration system rules. Reggies was given an F-1 designation, which meant he could go to school and work 20 hours a week. My daughter Thembi and I were assigned an F-2 as accompanying family members, and I was not allowed to work at all. We decided when we moved that we were going to do everything by the book. That meant no one would work and get paid under the table, as some immigrants did. We didn't know if we were going to be in the U.S. long term, but because of our faith and principles, we didn't want to break the law in any way.

At the outset, Reggies planned on attending Victory Bible Institute (VBI), which is a Bible school run by Victory Christian Center in Tulsa. Our I-20 student visa was actually issued by VBI. We arrived in the U.S. with nine pieces of luggage and $1,600, and we moved in with someone our American friend had connected us to. Our hostess picked us up from the airport, but to say it was a nightmare from the get-go is an understatement.

She did not realize how much of a responsibility it would be to have a couple and their child in her home. We stayed there for about two weeks because by the end of the first week, I began insisting we get an apartment and get out of there. The problem was we didn't have much money. Being from Zimbabwe, we didn't know we would have to pay first and last month's rent (and pay a utility deposit) since we had no credit history, and we only had $1,600. By the time we moved into that apartment, we had about $400 left. We had no blankets and nothing in the kitchen; in fact, we had nothing at all.

Back in Zimbabwe, our homes came with light fixtures. Here in the U.S., however, most apartments only have fixtures in the bathroom and the kitchen. It was summertime and the sun was setting and we told, our daughter, Thembi, to turn on the lights. When she flipped the switch, no lights came on, so Reggies had to go to Walmart to buy lamps along with a tablespoon, fork, teaspoon, bowl, and plate for each of us. That's how we started.

When Reggies went to VBI and looked at the curriculum, he realized the Bible school offered the same courses he had taken at the Hear the Word Bible School in Zimbabwe. We thought, *Why should he waste two years retaking courses he had already studied?* Because we came under the VBI-sponsored I-20 visa, we couldn't just up and leave the school. That's when we started to pray, asking God for direction.

Reggies would wake up every morning, go to the Oral Roberts University campus, which was walking distance from our apartment, walk around, and pray. One day, he bumped into a professor who asked where he was from and what he was doing there. After that meeting, the man helped him enroll in the education program at ORU. For a long time, VBI refused to release him from his I-20. They felt he had come to attend VBI, so why should they release him to go to ORU? For one month, he would go to class at ORU and I would be on my knees praying that God would move miraculously for VBI to release his I-20.

ORU was never sure they would accept Reggies into the master's in education program and had him on probation for the entire length of his master's program— even though he was a straight A student. We were blessed that my aunt, who helped raise me, was in education. Right after we got to the States, we asked her to follow up with the Harare Polytechnic and the University of Zimbabwe to get our transcripts sent over. ORU had a wonderful policy that if we were international and had an official transcript, the university would apply those credits to your degree. In my case, they applied my credits toward a four-year degree, so I had the equivalent of an associate's degree before I started to figure out my under-graduate plans. Reggies' transcript gave him an under-graduate degree, and he was able to enroll in the master's program—where he was on probation the entire time.

In Zimbabwe, I was a working professional with great benefits and profit sharing. I drove a company car and was an accomplished professional. I got here and based on my immigrant status, I was relegated to the category of an accompanying spouse. I went from a working profes-sional to a full-time housewife and mom. This was the first time I had been home 100% with our daughter, Thembi.

Back home, most of the working adults had nan-nies to care for their kids while they worked. That was a benefit of coming to the States, however, because I got to raise my own children who never had to stay in a daycare center. While that was a blessing, I lost and missed my professional role. While Reggies was growing in terms of making friends and establishing himself academically, I didn't have that opportunity.

There were many surprises when we moved to the States and we had to get used to many things that were quite different than what we were accustomed to.

For example, the commercialization of Christmas in America provided a massive culture shock for us. More than 18 years later, I still struggle with all the excess that comes with Christmas. Where we came from and the way I was raised, Christmas was about the birth of Christ, celebrated by having a wonderful meal with family. People traveled from different parts of Zimbabwe to meet, whether it was at Grandma's house or an uncle's home. Having a meal and spending time with your family were the highlights of the Christmas break, when *everything* shut down. Being in the U.S. and not having money to spend on anything was tough. The social pressure from seeing commercials and hearing people talk about stuff made that season difficult.

Later, when I enrolled at ORU around Christmas time, I had to say to my professor, "Can we stop talking about Christmas? As someone coming from a different culture, I am already overwhelmed by all of you talking about getting this, doing that, or spending money on this and that. Because the assumption I am getting is you think all of us can do or *want* to do those things."

For us, trying to secure a Christmas tree was traumatic due to the excessive commercialization of the holiday. Someone gave us one for our first Christmas here.

In subsequent years, I told Reggies I didn't even want a tree in the house. If you had a tree, then your child expected presents under it. We didn't have money for presents, so I figured we should not get a Christmas tree. It's only after living here for many years that we have established our own Christmas traditions. Every year, I still second-guess getting a tree and decorating the house.

The other challenging thing after moving to Tulsa was the number of immigrant families who lived there, including many Zimbabweans. One of the first students we met was a Zimbabwean pastor who had been living in the States for a long time. He and his family were very friendly and accommodating for new students and their families. I am from the Ndebele tribe but Reggies is from the Shona tribe, and most of the Zimbabweans we met were Shona-speaking families. It became clear to us early on that we wanted to limit our interactions with some Zimbabweans because there was much competition between them about what people were doing and what they had.

One of my earliest recollections was of the wives who couldn't understand why we weren't teaching our daughter Shona. I was surprised that some of the tribal tensions we experienced in Zimbabwe were showing up in America. We thought to ourselves, *If we were in Zimbabwe, would we be spending time with these people?* When we both answered no, we asked ourselves, *Why should we spend time with them now just because we are in the United States?* Some of our closest friends in Tulsa were from Kenya and Ghana.

Reggies finished his master's degree in about two years while serving as a grad assistant and working in the cafeteria at night. From the beginning to the end of his master's, he would write his assignments on a legal pad while he was at school, or at home in between jobs, and I would type them out. He graduated in May of 2002 and Kudzai, our son, was born in June. We managed to bring my mother to the States for his graduation since that was around the same time Kudzai was due. To show how precarious our financial situation was, we didn't even have money to buy a disposable camera to take pictures of Reggies' graduation. Therefore, we have no photos of his master's graduation from ORU. Following graduation, with the help of a friend's family, we celebrated with a lunch of corned beef and cabbage on rice.

I had a challenging pregnancy with both of my children since I suffered from morning sickness that lasted all day. With Thembi, I was hospitalized several times in the first three months. After we arrived in the States, we met a couple at Victory Church, who were physicians. When I started experiencing the same symptoms while pregnant with Kudzai, because we didn't have health insurance, they came to our apartment and were able to prescribe anti-nausea medication that helped with my symptoms. That was important because without health insurance, we couldn't afford my being hospitalized. In addition to these complications, both my children were induced, so I never had a normal labor progression.

Kudzai was two weeks overdue, so the doctor gave me a medicine meant to speed up the labor, but after the first twelve hours, I hadn't progressed at all. By the time they decided to give me the second dose, Reggies called friends to pray because both my oxygen levels and those of the baby were falling, too. I was placed on oxygen, which was not normal. We prayed and within two hours, Kudzai was born.

We rejoiced that we had our perfect family, a girl and a boy, but we were about to face some new mountains I described in the Introduction. The intensity of the challenges was overwhelming, and I am still learning how not to be lost in the needs we were about to face.

Chapter 8

Special Needs

We knew a couple in Tulsa who were physicians, and the wife was pregnant with her first child at the same time I was pregnant with our son, Kudzai. The first Thanksgiving after our children were born, we were invited to their house and they noticed Kudzai wasn't as bubbly or as communicative as their daughter who was the same age. A week or so later, the woman called and said she had been praying about how to tell us, but they had noticed Kudzai didn't seem to be reaching the verbal milestones expected for his age. They suggested asking our pediatrician some questions.

My first instinct was, *Oh my God, my baby isn't perfect*, and it took me another week to tell Reggies what they said. We started having our son's hearing checked and I took him in for testing six times over months, but they couldn't seem to get to the bottom of the problem. We eventually figured out his hearing was not the problem, and that's when the special services started for him. Thankfully, he qualified for state health insurance and we enrolled him in speech and occupational therapy.

During that time, I was the one who was home so I took on all the responsibilities of getting him to his doctor's and therapy appointments. Part of the state program for kids who had language delays was having speech and occupational therapists provide those services in the home. I was the one who was home with the therapist and did the homework assignments with our son. Looking back, the full responsibility for his special needs care rested with me. After every visit, I would report to Reggies what the doctor said and what we needed to do, but because he was in class pursuing his doctorate or at work, there were instances when they required decisions from us, and I made them there and then and told Reggies afterwards.

At that time, I was completing my undergraduate work in management at Oklahoma Wesleyan by going to school one night a week. I started that program when Kudzai was twelve months old. During this time, Kudzai had a few scary febrile seizures, which added another saga to his medical history. We didn't know if he had a seizure disorder or if the seizures were simply occurring because he was not feeling well and had a fever. At that point, I had to balance being a wife, mom, and student. I was also involved in things outside the home like volunteering for Head Start, our daughter's preschool program, and serving as a board member of a policy council for Tulsa County Community Action Project, the organization that ran Head Start.

To be honest, at that time I never thought about whether I was fulfilled as a person or a woman. I was responding to life and circumstances the way I was raised back in Zimbabwe where fulfillment was not something we spent much time considering. I did what was before me, but as I look back, I was searching for something, otherwise why would I have been going to school and serving in the community?

I saw my husband was heading towards a job in higher education because his doctorate was in higher education administration, but I didn't know what that looked like at the time. In 2006, I graduated with my degree and that's when we got our work permits from the U.S. government. I started looking for a job right away and applied for one with a group called The Voice of Martyrs. That was right after we bought our first house when Kudzai was in a language emersion program in Broken Arrow, Oklahoma.

This was a full-time job with benefits, but I initially turned them down because it was based in Bartlesville, 45 minutes from Tulsa and we didn't think it would be wise for us to uproot and move. We had just bought the house, I had just started graduate school, and Kudzai was in his program. The other reason I turned them down was because I had also just started a management trainee program with Walgreens. With my retail and PR background from Zimbabwe, they thought I was a good fit for their management trainee program. To say it was the least exciting thing I have done in the U.S. so far, is an understatement. It was nothing more than tedious and because I spent most of my time at work on my feet, my nerve-damaged leg was swollen and hurt every day. I was miserable!

The trajectory of a Walgreens' career was to train as a store manager in all departments and also become certified as a pharmacy technician while learning how to manage the entire store. Once people graduated from the program in a year and a half to two years, they were then assigned their own store to manage. It seemed like a great opportunity based on my past retail experience, as well as the company's lucrative profit sharing, but I didn't enjoy it at all.

Another reason why I didn't enjoy the work and started second-guessing my decision to join the company was that, during the interview, the regional manager made it clear that while they supported their employees getting undergraduate degrees, he said Walgreens did not see the need for or support employees wanting to pursue post-graduate studies. I joined the company a few weeks after I had started the Master's in Human Relations degree at the University of Oklahoma. That was a red flag because I knew that I wanted to go beyond my undergraduate degree.

Thankfully, the Voice of the Martyrs (VOM) called back to offer a moving allowance and several other incentives. I later found out that the gentleman who was to become my boss had prayed for someone who had international experience and had lived in another country other than the U.S. because he had been raised as a pastor's kid in Papua New Guinea. He knew that because VOM worked with people from various cultural backgrounds, having that experience was beneficial. Part of my job was interviewing persecuted Christians and pastors from around the world. He thought my experience and expertise would not only be an asset to his department, but also to the entire organization.

When they asked me to come for a second interview, they gave me a writing assignment, which was to watch a DVD and write a news story about a Bangladeshi pastor who had suffered persecution. Following the assignment, my boss looked over my work, went back into his office, and told the Lord I was the person he wanted to have this job. He prayed for God to move on my heart to accept the position because he felt I would be a great fit. Later, we took the offer and that was the most amazing experience I have had since working in the U.S.—and an important step in my purpose journey.

Working for VOM was an amazing experience because I believed in what the organization was doing and I was making a difference. I had responsibility for telling the stories of persecuted believers from around the world, which would not be known by the American public, if we didn't tell them. That was quite gratifying. I was making a difference, not only for them, but helped spread the gospel by sharing their amazing faith.

The highlight of my experience with the VOM was when they sent me to northern Nigeria in 2008. I had informed them we were moving because Reggies had received a job offer, but my boss said he didn't think anyone could tell the stories of the widows, orphans, and persecuted Christians from Nigeria like I would be able to do. That's why he sent me to Nigeria to interview the widows whose husbands had been killed because they were believers.

On the second day of interviewing, I sat with two women who were married to brothers. They told me of the gruesome murders of their husbands and explained how they hid because Muslim extremists had set fire to their houses. All journalism protocol aside, I left the room and broke done crying. It was not an elegant cry, but one those ugly cries with deep sobs. While growing up in Zimbabwe, I had no idea that such brutality was happening on the African continent. I had to come to the States and then go to Kano, Nigeria to learn about persecution occurring close to where I was born and raised.

My career, as gratifying and life-changing as it was, however, was on a collision course with family duties, for our son's problems were about to intensify while Reggies' career took a major step upward. There was nothing for me to do but to surrender my career aspirations to the needs of my family. I thought I knew what that meant until I had to face circumstances beyond my worst nightmare, which I will describe in the next chapter.

Chapter 9

Misdiagnosed

When I went to Nigeria, I had just started my PhD at the University of Oklahoma and Reggies had just graduated with his Doctorate in Education and was looking for a job in higher education administration. When I traveled to Nigeria in April 2009, he was working at Southwestern Christian University in Bethany, Oklahoma near Oklahoma City, having started in December 2008. While I was in Nigeria, he was commuting between Bartlesville and Bethany, which was a distance of about 150 miles. At that point, I was going to school full-time, working full time, and caring for both kids who were just finishing up their school year in Bartlesville where we had lived for three years. To put Reggies closer to his work, we moved to Edmond in May 2009.

Prior to our family moving, my boss at The Voice of the Martyrs asked me if I wanted to work remotely from Edmond between June 2009 to December 2010. VOM was building a new headquarters and my boss didn't want to hire somebody new during the transition. I worked remotely under contract and drove to Bartlesville from Edmond twice a month.

During this same time, I was working as a graduate assistant at the University of Oklahoma (OU Tulsa Campus). That meant that in addition to driving to Bartlesville twice a month, I also drove to Tulsa three times a week. I had this crazy schedule until 2011 when my grad assistantship was canceled.

When I finished my commitment with The Voice of the Martyrs in 2011 and I shifted my focus to completing my doctorate, it was around the same time that Kudzai's challenges were becoming more pronounced. While balancing classes at both Tulsa and Norman campuses, my role at home became taking care of and managing Kudzai at school and also taking care of and managing home because Reggies was about to enter his new position. I graduated from OU in 2012 and Reggies became president at Southwestern Christian University in 2012 as well.

Kudzai was having issues with sleep, not sleeping for long periods of time, which would affect his behavior.

Because of this I had forego sleep sometimes so Reggies could sleep since he had to go to work. What I didn't realize then but do now is that I needed sleep too because I was working during the day. I was emailing teachers, being called about his behavior and having that on my mind all day and night.

That was the beginning of me taking on more than what I should have instead of Reggies and I equally managing that situation. Now I observe the way Kudzai is attached to me, and it's to the point when I'm sitting on the couch, he can't sit across from me, he has to sit right next to me—sometimes even leaning on me. He is a big boy, weighing more than 220 pounds, and during that time of his transition, I was the one who was always there for and with him. Maybe if we had divided that time more evenly and effectively, he would not be as attached to me as he is now.

Reggies was a college president, and I wanted to find a job in higher education too, but no one wanted to hire the "first lady" from another university so I never applied for a job anywhere. I also became more and more absorbed in my family situation at home. When puberty hit for Kudzai, his care consumed me for the next few years.

Every year, we were invited to take part in the graduation ceremonies at Rhema Bible School in Tulsa. In 2015, Reggies had also planned a ministry trip for his university athletes to the nation of Colombia. The Friday night before we were to leave for Colombia we went to graduation and left Thembi and Kudzai with a babysitter. I checked in before the commencement started and everything was fine. I checked in just before we left Tulsa and everything was still fine. I called home at the end of night and everything was fine. As we were driving home, however, I got a call from Thembi telling me that Kudzai had become aggressive.

After we got home and everything had calmed down, I thought about it and didn't think I should go on the trip. My personality style does tend to be pessimistic and Reggies' style is the exact opposite. He reminded me we had planned the trip for a long time and I needed a break. I was thinking, *Kudzai's disruption and aggression are happening before we leave and only God knows what will happen after we leave.* I eventually agreed to go but on one condition: I had to keep my cell phone on for the duration of the trip in case the kids needed to get in touch with us.

To show you how normalized abnormal stuff was at that point, I left with a colleague to drive to Dallas to catch our flight to Colombia. Reggies had a speaking engagement in Tennessee so he had left the day before I did and was going to come on a different flight to meet us in Colombia. We flew from Dallas to Florida and met up with our students and faculty going with us so we could all fly to Barranquilla, Colombia.

I was at breakfast our first morning in Colombia when I received a call to find out that things at home were crazy. Reggies was on his way and had not arrived yet. I sat in my hotel room talking to a police officer at our home where my daughter was frantic on a speakerphone along with the sitter. I merged my calls from Colombia with a psychologist trying to figure out what to do. It's by the grace of God that I insisted I keep my phone on when we left. I spent that first morning coordinating care for our son from Colombia. While this was going on, I was looking for flights to get back home if I needed to. All this before our mission even started.

I called our friend Jim and asked him if he would meet Kudzai and Thembi at the hospital so we would know we had someone there we could trust. Then we called our friends from Malawi who were visiting the States and asked them if they could go to our house. That way we would have them there to evaluate the situation. By the time Reggies arrived at noon, thinking everything was fine and normal, I had gone to pieces because everything had exploded.

I had to manage the trip and that experience, the situation at home, medications, calling home, and arranging for Thembi to stay someplace else for the night so at least she could feel safe. I stayed the whole time in Colombia but had already planned to go home a few days before Reggies. The psychologist assured me that we had support at home and advised me to stay in Colombia for my own well-being.

In 2015, Kudzai's aggressive episodes got so bad that we had to make the decision to have him in the hospital for seven days, which occurred right after Reggies had left on another trip. We had both gone maybe two or three nights without sleep. The morning he was leaving to go on that trip, we had called for support from the crisis intervention officers three times in a 24-hour period. The night before our son was admitted to the hospital, an officer came to the house at 4 AM because I had to barricade myself in a part of the house while Kudzai was in another part. This was the same officer who had been there the night before. When he asked where my husband and daughter were, I told him he was on a trip and Thembi was at a friend's house to get a break. He looked at me and said, "Who's giving you a break?"

He then said because he had been to our home

three times, the law did not allow him to leave me alone with Kudzai, so he gave two options. I either had to call someone to come be with me or we had to call the ambulance and take our son to the emergency room. I chose the ambulance. I drove behind the ambulance and when we arrived at the emergency room, they only hooked him up to a few monitors because it wasn't an acute injury.

I reported that he was on the autism spectrum and was having aggressive episodes, informing them that a neuropsychologist was caring for him. The nurse handed me a sheet of paper with mental health services listed and informed me that kids on the spectrum had to be cared for by a psychiatrist. I did not know that and asked if I could call someone right then. She said everyone was gone and would not be back until Monday. They asked for my co-pay and sent me home.

I came to the conclusion that this was how a parent could come to the hospital, seek help, not get it, go home, only to have the child injure or kill the parent. It was about 4:30 AM on a Saturday when we left the hospital. I had kept the number of the neuropsychologist, who was spending a couple of days at her lake house (part of my profile is to pay attention to details, thank God). Later that day, I called and said there was no way we could continue to live like this. I asked what our options were in terms of having him admitted as an inpatient to get him some help.

The psychologist told me I would need a referral and she would make some calls to see if there were any facilities that could handle our son's medical needs. She called back to inform me she had found a facility in Tulsa, an hour-and-a-half away, and if I drove him there, they were willing to help. She advised me not to make the drive alone in case I needed support on the way, so I called a pastor friend (our daughters were friends) who had experience handling mental health emergencies. This friend was none other than Cari, my now best friend. When I called and asked her to accompany me, without hesitating, she was at my house to help in whatever way I needed her.

I had no choice but to drive from Oklahoma City to Tulsa and sign papers to have my child admitted to a mental health facility by myself because my husband was out of town, and I could not wait for him to return. I was into doing whatever needed to be done but I was thoroughly exhausted. I had to get our son to a safe place and let the professionals take over from there. He was in that hospital for seven days.

Having him admitted inpatient helped because they took him off all medications. One of several traumatic experiences I went through by myself related to our son when we first got him to the neuropsychologist and she conducted what are supposed to be diagnostic screenings. Our initial appointment was to be Reggies and I completing self-report evaluations. Reggies asked her if he needed to be there for the follow-up appointment, which was her evaluation one-on-one with our son. She said no and stressed that it would be beneficial for him to attend the third appointment because that's when she would give us the results of the screening. He only needed to be present for that one.

Individuals on the autism spectrum can't be tested in conventional ways. Their skills are different from the neuro-typical individuals. One of the things that kids on the spectrum do is talk to themselves—a lot. It's what some speech therapists call scripting or stimming.

Therapists believe this is partly self-soothing and helps alleviate anxiety. For our son, who developed speech late, scripting was non-stop and when he became anxious, he raised his voice.

When he reached puberty and hormones and chemical changes in his body began, this resulted in negative behaviors and incidents of aggression increased. During this time, his scripting was loud and non-stop, mainly about his favorite television shows, his guitars (especially the Jonas Brothers). He has always had the ability to recall movie scenes word for word. With all this going on, the neuropsychologist tried to administer a test, but she could not get him to focus and answer questions because he was scripting, talking about his guitars, his music, and whatever he was interested in. That caused the psychologist to produce a diagnosis labeling Kudzai with childhood onset schizophrenia.

Contrary to her previous reassurance, she decided to deliver the diagnosis the same day of the "testing" when I was in her office without Reggies. Later when our son was admitted to the hospital, I had to complete a big pile of paperwork and the psychiatrist at the inpatient facility asked me who gave him the diagnosis of childhood onset schizophrenia. I told him the doctor who was our neuropsychologist had done so. They asked me to sign a release to obtain the testing to see what criteria she had used to come to that conclusion. The psychiatrist informed us they had a room full of kids who had schizophrenia and Kudzai didn't exhibit any of the symptoms. They told us our son was exhibiting autistic behavior. I called the neuropsychologist to request the release of her results to the hospital. It is many years later, and I am I still waiting.

In addition to the misdiagnosis, the psychologist referred him to an Advanced Practice Registered Nurse who loaded him up with strong antipsychotic medications, which built up in his system, complicating his problems. That's how we ended up with the continued aggressive episodes and his admission into a mental health facility.

Many of those days are a blur in my memory, and searching for personal meaning and purpose was out of the question. I knew, and Reggies knew, I needed to get away, so in the fall of 2015, I went to Zimbabwe to visit my mother. This was my first time back to Zimbabwe since we had left and my first trip alone. I sat in the airport in Oklahoma City waiting for my flight out I could not believe I could choose to listen to a podcast or read a book. I had an eight-hour layover in London Heathrow before my flight to South Africa. That was like heaven on earth for me because I could sit and watch people, get myself a drink, listen to music, or read a book. I could do anything I wanted. It was refreshing and different to not be the one taking care of everybody but just being, and just taking care of myself for a change.

I was in Zimbabwe for a week. I was able to see my mom, uncle, aunt, and my mom's two older sisters. I saw some cousins and my aunt took me to my grandmother's grave and house where I grew up. On that trip I was shocked to see how Zimbabwe had changed compared to when we left.

There is a stigma attached to mental illness in Africa and this was the first time I could explain to all of them in detail concerning Kudzai's diagnosis and some of the challenges we had been facing. It was also the first time I could have an honest discussion with not only my mom but my uncle about the affect Kudzai's sickness had had on me. I told them I had been diagnosed with depression, anxiety and insomnia, and I was taking medication (I continue to take medication).

It was also good for me to be that open with them and for them to know that when they called or wrote to check on us, they had some idea what was going on with us in our world. Being that vulnerable and open with them has improved how I relate with them. When I text them and ask for prayer because he's having problems, they can know exactly how to pray. It was difficult to communicate these things over the phone and the person-to-person interaction was the best way.

In Zimbabwe when someone asks you something or makes a suggestion, it's not because they want to hear your response. Sometimes they are just talking but not really interested in hearing your opinion. In America, we are taught to be assertive. When someone asks a question, they are expecting information in return. For example, I had a cousin raised by my grandmother who was about to get married. I was giving him some sisterly advice on his upcoming marriage when he said, "Oh, you're very opinionated," and I thought, *Yes I am!*

The person my family saw when I visited was different from the person they knew when I left. I was also different from the one they thought I would become. Living in the U.S. had certainly changed me, and without a doubt, it was consistent with who I truly was and a part of finding myself. I had made more progress than I thought, but I had to step away from my world in the U.S. to see it.

I found myself able to communicate with my elders differently. I was very forthright and frank. I certainly was not a typical woman in their forties back home in Zimbabwe. Speaking up the way I did is not common in Zimbabwe. Some of those things I said most women there would keep to themselves.

Even though I was only there for a week, I was brokenhearted to see where my country had gone and how it had deteriorated. Perhaps it was because I had a new country and a new perspective, but it was also because of leadership decisions by government officials that had cost the residents much in the way of economic security and growth. My week went by all too quickly and soon it was time to return home and continue the journey to find my purpose while also diving back into the situation from which I had enjoyed only a short respite. It was time to face the realities again at home.

Chapter 10

Intervention

We have always known that our son had unique challenges from when he was a year old, but when he hit puberty, like every teenager, his hormones kicked in and with it, puberty compounded his challenges and resulted in behavioral problems at school and home. These varied from visible anxiety to serious episodes of aggression, which included hitting, kicking, and a lack of self-control we had not seen before.

What has been mind boggling to us and our doctors

is that kids on the autism spectrum generally exhibit aggression from a young age and yet with our son, the aggressive behaviors were delayed. Although our son exhibited developmental delays early, he was not diagnosed with autism spectrum disorders until after he was eight years old. Of course, the autism spectrum is very wide, so every child with autism is different. Their behaviors, uniqueness, and challenges are also different. Meanwhile, parenting a child with a disability is not for the faint of heart, notwithstanding a child with a spectrum of challenges and a myriad of atypical behaviors.

In September 2016, my husband had just returned from a week-long business and ministry trip, going once again to Colombia. While he was gone, I faced more challenges with our son who was now 14 years old. During my husband's trip, Kudzai once again had episodes of aggression, impulsivity, and anxiety. He does not do well with changes in his routine or change in general, so when my husband or I travel, he exhibits harmful behaviors both at home and at school.

When my husband got home from this trip, I was emotionally and physically exhausted. I was depleted and barely holding on. Normally when my husband travels, we talk by phone and Skype several times a day, so while on the trip, he knew what was going on at home. During one of those calls, I started crying uncontrollably and I kept repeating, "I can't live like this anymore." I had tried my best to be and appear strong when he called, but I could not put on a facade anymore. I was struggling.

I had experienced days when our son impulsively hit or kicked me, and it was nearly impossible to redirect him or gently encourage him to do day-to-day tasks that many parents take for granted. In the past when my husband traveled, I had challenges with our son, but this trip was excruciatingly painful and the episodes were non-stop. Complicating the situation was that I was also having trouble sleeping and eating, and I was understandably anxious most of the day. Unfortunately, my son picked up on my increased anxiety and that in turn increased his anxiety levels and so we were in a vicious cycle.

The night my husband arrived home, he asked if we could sit down and have a talk. He had intuitively listened to our conversations during the many telephone calls during the trip and saw my demeanor when he got back home, so he knew I was struggling. He asked me how I was doing and I told him I was exhausted both physically and emotionally, which is normal after days of caring for our son on my own without a break. My husband went on to explain that when he travels, he worries more about me than he does about our son.

I was surprised by that statement, partly because I did not fully understand it. Also, my perception was he worried more about our son and his many challenges. He went on to tell me that he was concerned because I was not taking care of myself physically, emotionally, and spiritually, and that I had, in essence, lost myself. Anyone who knows me can attest to the fact that I have always put others before myself. I usually let people know when I don't like something, but I will quickly shut down and not engage further. I also tend to shut down and retreat within myself when I am tired.

He suggested that although in the last two years our son's behavioral challenges had made going anywhere, let alone church, impossible, I needed to re-engage with others outside the home and go to church whenever I could. He encouraged me to reach out to and interact with people. With a concerned look in his eyes that I had never seen before, he said he felt that if something tragic was ever to happen to him, he was worried I wouldn't have anyone close to me to call because I was isolated.

I sat there and respectfully listened to him. Part of me resonated with what he was saying because in the past I had also asked myself many questions about where I was in life. As important as it is to care for my husband and kids, especially our son who needed extra support, I hoped that this was not how it would be for most of my future. I had nights when I cried myself to sleep because of exhaustion and pain from our son's aggression and I wondered how my life had come to this.

While my husband was on that trip, I sat on the couch after one aggressive episode and asked myself a myriad of questions: *Where was God in all this hurt? Why was this happening to me? How could I continue to live like this and still be a functioning wife to my husband and mother to both our children? How would I be able to feign having the energy to be resilient, keep going, and seem to have things under control to those around me, who had no idea what was going on? Most importantly, how could I stay spiritually engaged with God when it felt like my prayers were bouncing off the ceiling?* I felt as if the more I read the Bible and prayed, the worse things got.

As hard as it was to hear my loving husband, my best friend, and a man I respect telling me that I had lost myself, it was what I needed to hear. In hindsight, I needed someone else to validate what I was already feeling inside. I knew his concern was coming from a loving place and that he had my best interests at heart. Deep down, his words resonated within me because he was right. I had lost myself and felt isolated. I had developed resentment and anger towards God and those around me. I was not a fun person to be around.

I was resentful because I felt I was the only one taking on most of the responsibility of care for our son. When it came time to talk to doctors, I was the one. When teachers called about behavioral issues, they talked to me. When the assistant principal called to tell me Kudzai had struck another student and was suspended, I was the one who got the news first. I had internalized so much that sometimes I couldn't breathe. The worst thing you can say to someone who was where I was emotionally was to say, "How do you do it?" or "Bless your heart, I'll pray for you." Those words, though noble, were annoying.

During my husband's trip to Colombia, I also resented that he had a chance to travel, have a restful night's sleep, and got to have fun. In contrast, my reality was that I was on edge most of the day when our son's mood was off kilter. My husband rarely picked him up from school and so he did not get to talk to teachers and hear a litany of all the things that had gone wrong during the day, which at this point included aggressive, hurtful behavior.

Don't misunderstand me. My husband is a loving, compassionate, and supportive person who works hard for our family and has our best interests at heart. When he was traveling, he was faithful to check in from time to time, while I was at home. I had grown to resent that his career was progressing and he was helping advance the careers of his staff, however, while I was stagnant and had become a full-time caregiver. This realization surprised me because I am his greatest supporter, but I also realized that because I had no outlet to do anything except deal with problems, my thoughts and feelings started to be absorbed by those problems and my inner dialogue was derailed by negative thinking. Therefore, when my husband told me I had lost myself, I thought, *Duh, of course I have lost myself. Who wouldn't living like this?*

I wasn't living life. I was alive and breathing, but I was coasting from one crisis to another. During good days, instead of appreciating a break from the chaos and smelling the roses, I was miserable and wondering when the next crisis would come. This was an exhausting way to live. What was interesting is that although I had these feelings and thoughts bottled up, I did not openly share them with my husband because I did not want to seem selfish and insensitive. In hindsight, considering everything I was going through, this seems ludicrous, but in my exhausted, foggy state of mind, this made total sense. I realized then that suppressing such important things is not healthy for myself and definitely not productive for our marriage.

When we became parents, we dedicated both our children to God when they were toddlers. Since then, we have raised them in a God-fearing home. We trusted God for and through every milestone in our children's lives and viewed our role as parents to be stewards of the two gifts God had given to us. As they were growing up, we made a concerted effort to instill godly character and a biblical foundation in their lives. In past years when we had serious medical challenges with our son, God visibly intervened and healed him, so for many months, I had grappled with how a loving, healing God could allow our family to be going through this painful and traumatic time. I was in a very dark place.

As the saying goes, "I would not wish this on my worst enemy." I felt lost, hopeless, helpless, and trapped. The atmosphere around me was always tense and when we were all home, we were anxious. There were times my husband and I got into arguments because I was exhausted, frustrated, and had shut down emotionally. On some of these occasions, he was frustrated because he felt I was developing a "martyr's complex." He thought I felt like I was the only one suffering because of our son's challenges and behaviors, and I felt I was on the receiving end of most of our son's aggression.

Sometimes he did not understand what I was trying to tell him. We still have moments when I wonder if he fully understands what I have gone through and sometimes still go through. When it came to care for our son, I felt I was doing all the heavy lifting. If anything needed to be done, I had to do it. Up to this point, I was taking our son to doctor's appointments by myself and these were challenging visits that left both my son and I exhausted. I needed a break.

While I understood my husband had a highly stressful full-time job, I had willingly taken on most of the hands-on responsibilities at home and now needed him at times to pick up the slack. In hindsight, this was an interesting position to be in because I took on most of the responsibility and when it became too much, I lost myself and could not shake the darkness I was in. I needed a respite that wasn't forthcoming.

For two years, my life had been an exhausting blur, littered with sporadic episodes of quiet, while always anticipating something else going wrong. My once vibrant life had slipped away. The professional dreams I once had were hijacked by the need to care for our son. Each day when I dropped him off at school, I was anxious, teetering on the brink of a breakdown. From time to time, I found myself asking how I got here. I had so many questions, but few answers.

For the first time in my adult life, I was experiencing a crisis of faith and life. *How do I continue to be like Christ when things are falling apart? How do I remain strong for my family, while I feel like I am treading water and can barely keep from drowning? How could my husband be traveling the world preaching, lives being changed, and at the same time facing challenges at home that seem insurmountable and for which we had no answers? How did I get here? Here I am living in the United States of America, I am educated, I have achieved what some call "the American Dream." We had financial stability and yet, I had lost myself in life. How did this happen in America, the land of endless opportunities and dreams?*

If you think I have answered all these questions and you are looking for a book that ends with rainbows and butterflies, I apologize in advance because you will be disappointed. I have not figured it all out, but I am grateful that I am on a journey of self-discovery. I am truly a work in progress. I was lost and am on a journey of re-discovery.

I took my husband's intervention to heart. I had to make some changes. They were small at the time, but they have made a big difference in my progress to where I am today. He has taken on more responsibility. Kudzai is older and our move to a new city has helped because we have more land where we live and better support services for him. Let me share with you in the next few chapters some of the significant events that have let me know progress on my personal development is happening, but still at times at a snail's pace compared to what I would want and think I need it to be.

Chapter 11

Fears

I have often reflected on the concept of fear and the role it has played in my life. I now realize that I have lived in fear all my life—fear of being found out when I disobeyed the rules; fear of not being good enough to fulfill family expectations; fear of change caused by not living in one place with the same people for all my life and being passed around the family from uncle to uncle; fear of my secrets being revealed.

When we moved to the U.S., my immigration status was as an accompanying spouse. I had no legal standing whatsoever and I was not permitted to work. During that time, my fear of losing Reggies was great. *What if something happened to him? What would happen to me and my child?* As students studying in the U.S., we didn't have life or health insurance, or any other safety net. I learned how to access free resources while trusting in the Lord.

One of the first things I did was determine which universities had medical schools and which medical schools had clinics. When I took Thembi to the doctor before we had Kudzai, they would charge us on a sliding scale based on Reggies' income—or lack of it. I frequented food pantries even though Reggies didn't like that because where we came from, people didn't go to food pantries. For me, it was a matter of how we could supplement our income because we didn't have much. One Christmas, I went and got a Salvation Army basket and gifts for Thembi.

Later while in grad school, I volunteered as an intern for the Salvation Army board and I was a person ringing the bell to raise money for other people. I was a bell ringer in one of the wealthiest sections of Tulsa, standing there thinking that it was a full-circle moment because I was raising money for people in need after they had helped us years earlier during our Christmas crisis.

Then came fear of what was going on with Kudzai. *What does his future look like?* This fear still rears its ugly head from time to time. There was also the fear of not being able to be a "good wife" based on our cultural norms. *What will our relationship look like having a marriage with all these stressors of work, school, children, and financial lack?* I was afraid because of some of my own health challenges. The snake bite I described earlier has caused long-term neuropathy in my right leg.

A couple years ago, I looked into whether I could have some type of reconstruction to relieve the problems I face with my leg because when it is warm or cold outside, my leg swells. When I travel long distances in a car or plane, it swells. For that reason, I have a handicapped sticker on my car. If I walk too far, it swells. If I exercise too much, it swells. After living with this for years, a neurologist informed me I had neuropathy in my leg. Because I wasn't taking good care of my emotional health, I developed other physical ailments. I had to have a hysterectomy in 2014 because of fibroids. I've had bladder infections and have been so stressed at times that my immune system was completely compromised.

I am learning to acknowledge that fear exists and then dig into the Bible to find help in addressing the fear—yes, I did begin to pursue God more earnestly after the talk with my husband. That has helped and I have used prayer as a first line of defense. In my case, I find that writing things down has helped me see them for what they are. All these fears haven't come to me at the same time, but during different phases of my life.

I don't want to give the impression that it's only deciding to meditate on Scripture and prayer that have helped. It's being conscious and self-aware of how I am feeling—and admitting it to myself and my husband. *Is that a rational feeling I am having? Or am I now connecting the dots to go down a rabbit hole I cannot get out of? Do I need to share this with someone?* I have found the more I think and start verbalizing certain things, the more real they become in my life—good or bad. When I do that, those things begin to manifest in my life and emotions. Reading

God's word and holding myself in check through the word of God has been a great help.

Psalm 126:5 has been helpful: "Those who plant in tears will harvest with shouts of joy." For me, crying is a release. For a long time, I associated crying with weakness, and I have no idea why. I have found that if I am able to cry it out, I feel better. I am planting in tears, so therefore I am going to reap with joy. That is encouraging to me.

Then there is John 10:10: "The thief comes only to steal, kill, and destroy. I have come that they may have life and have it in full." It helps to identify that some of my fears are coming from the enemy of my soul. For example, if in the past Kudzai had a good week, and then we have an incident at school, the default reaction would be, *Oh my God, we are going back to the way things used to be.* I have been taking those thoughts captive and I am saying, *No, let me praise God for how far we have come. These are the milestones we have reached. This is just a bump in the road as we go to where God wants to take us.*

I have found that framing my thoughts is important. I must put my thoughts in context and just like a bad frame can ruin a good picture, so can a bad frame ruin a legitimate thought. A good frame can also make a mediocre picture better, so it's crucial that I work to frame my thoughts and keep a proper perspective. I have to look at how far we have come as opposed to the fear that we are going back. First John 4:18 states that perfect love casts out fear. Fear implies punishment, so my fear is a barometer of my love relationship with the Lord. I have found that I am afraid to acknowledge my fears, because then I feel I am deficient spiritually and therefore I am disqualified from any of God's blessings. My legalistic religious upbringing contributed to that thought. Psalm 56:4 has also been helpful: "I trust in God, so why should I be afraid?"

It's interesting how I can be hesitant to pray even though prayer is a great help to me. I can be especially hesitant when praying for things I have prayed about before. It's like I think God is too busy giving Bentleys and Mini Coopers to other people to hear my prayer that I have already prayed. Therefore, He can't hear my meagre mundane prayer. I have had to press through that and, just like the psalmist, pour out my heart to the Lord again and again.

Another fear I recorded in my diary recently was about the state of my professional career. *What services are available for Kudzai that would provide a respite for me? How do I prioritize myself and continue the journey of self-discovery? Is there a job for me somewhere?* I fear getting back into a downward emotional spiral. Based on what I know about my personality profile, I know that if something needs to be done, I will step forward and do it. That means I tend to overextend myself, and then not say anything when that happens. I have to step forward less and I am doing so.

I am struggling to find my purpose, the essence of who I am. It's difficult to think in those terms when my life seems so unstable and uncertain. I have thought about being self-employed, but what does that look like? I am not skilled to sell anything to anyone, so it could not be in sales. I could consult because my resume indicates that I have a wide swath of knowledge on different subjects, but how do I find the clients?

I am a person of color, but not an American (I am a citizen), and there are not a lot of people like me who have a foot in Africa and a foot in the U.S. I have considered how I could help the academic world better serve people like me, a first-generation international student coming from Africa. I could also help adult learners from a diverse background.

If you ask me what I am passionate about, I am passionate about social justice. That means diversity, inclusion, and equity. My family loves watching Andrew Zimmern on the Travel Channel and Anthony Bourdain on CNN, who takes us to Iran, Vietnam, or Kenya each hour and we learn about unique people, cuisine, and history. I love platforms that give exposure to everybody and not monolithic situations where the focus is on one group of people.

My doctoral dissertation was on ethnic and gender diversity. I studied three human service organizations: the Girl Scouts of America, the Red Cross, and the Salvation Army. I examined the literature on diversity in human service organizations, and conducted my own empirical qualitative research using one-on-one interviews with randomly-selected board members of those organizations. I also examined board documents and sponsored focus groups with board members. One would think a human-service organization serving minorities would have people on the boards who represent the population it serves. That is not always the case.

What I found is that the recruiting methods for obtaining board members do not lend themselves to be open to everybody. Thus, the people they are serving are not represented on the board. I also discovered their documents do not reflect people who look differently than they do, who are of a different gender or color. For example, the third organization I looked at was the Girl Scouts of America. It was interesting to see that it was the only organization that had male board members, even though it is an organization serving girls. It made me wonder if the Boy Scouts have women on their board. I never studied them, so I don't know. Some of my recommendations in my dissertation were recommending steps a board can take to increase their diversity.

I am a person of color and I believe that when I walk into a room, I come with valuable ideas. I am smart and articulate, and I can help make a difference. I consider myself a social justice advocate because I speak concerning issues about which I am passionate. For example, I went through a season where I was a court-appointed special advocate for the county in which we lived. I had four neglected kids as part of my caseload, and my job was to go into court and tell the judge whether the parents had it together or not.

The meaning of an advocate is a person who publicly supports or recommends a particular cause or policy. Social justice addresses issues like the distribution of wealth, opportunities, and privileges within a society. All those have been issues I have been interested in since my days as a journalist. When I worked for a nonprofit in Zimbabwe, I was the only woman on the reporting staff. I covered a lot of the health issues, and I wrote articles educating people on HIV/AIDS, which was a big issue at that time in Zimbabwe. I worked with women's organizations, talking about socioeconomic issues impacting women. When Zimbabwe was going through their land redistribution process, I sat in on meetings with the Minister of Lands to see how women could be included in the land redistribution.

As I write, I am encouraging myself that I have made progress. I have asked good questions and held on to those questions until I got answers, or at least greater understanding. I am not where I want or need to be, but I am not where I was. My trip home to Zimbabwe was important in my self-discovery process and there are a few other recent trips that have made a difference in my life. Let me share those with you now.

Chapter 12

A Weekend of Firsts

After all I have been through, after I returned from my trip to Zimbabwe, I soon forgot what it was like to have time for myself where I could make decisions based on what I wanted. My husband encouraged me to accept the invitation from my two cousins in Chicago to visit them and my young niece. These cousins are the children of my aunt's youngest sister—the aunt married to my uncle who raised me. That uncle was my mother's second oldest brother, the one who remarried, so I guess his wife is my step-aunt, if there is such a title. This was the first time as an adult I planned and took a trip that had no agenda, only an opportunity to see my cousins and have fun. I call that trip a weekend of firsts because during the weekend, I got to experience a variety of exciting things for the first time.

I had come to associate my son as the one who had separation anxiety when we were apart, but I realized I had developed it too when I am away from him. As excited as I was about the trip, the week before the trip some feelings of doubt crept in a few days before my departure as I wondered if taking the trip was the best thing for me to do. I reconsidered my decision to go—but only briefly—as I processed feelings of being selfish, but I am learning there are times I need to be a bit selfish—at least by my definition—and do things for myself. My husband has always encouraged me to participate in things that excite me and help me express my individuality, but in recent years I had neglected this important part of living life. My husband and I planned my trip to Chicago for more than eight months and on my departure day, I was giddy with excitement, anticipation, and all the possibilities of the coming fun.

In the past, I had visited Chicago for a conference and traveled through its airports in transit many times, but I had not visited the sites and seen all the wonderful things the city had to offer. The day before the trip, my cousin asked me if I was open to taking public transit from the airport to her apartment because of Chicago traffic. I was apprehensive to do so because I was unsure how far I would have to walk and did not want to start the trip by aggravating the neuropathy in my leg. I was also a little nervous because I had never been on public transit in a big city before. We nixed that idea and when I arrived on a Thursday afternoon, my cousin and niece picked me up from the airport in her car. My second cousin who lives in Ohio was working, so she drove to Chicago on Friday night.

The drive home from the airport was informative because my cousin took the long way home due to traffic so she gave me a driving tour of all the sights and neighborhoods in the northern part of Chicago. It was an exciting drive. Prior to my visit, my niece put together a list of all the restaurants to which she wanted to take me. As we drove through some neighborhoods, she would get excited and point out certain places, but would catch herself and revert to using code words so she would not spoil the surprises she had in store for me. That was sweet and cute.

My cousin has lived in Chicago for more than ten years as I write. She moved there from Ohio to go to school and graduated with her master's degree from DePaul University. She now works in the information technology field. My cousins and niece usually visited our family every Christmas, but in recent years, we had cancelled their visit because our son wasn't feeling well. As a result, I had not seen them in nearly three years, and that's why we were all thrilled to have an opportunity to reconnect.

During the first night, I kept wondering why I hadn't made the trip to visit them before and I was reminded of the verse, "And we know that in all things God works for the good of those who love him, who have been called according to his purpose" (Romans 8:28). I believe God's timing is perfect and that my visit to Chicago happened when it did because I was ready to enjoy it and willing to experience and embrace new things.

My first night in Chicago we decided to go to Nandos, Portuguese, chicken restaurant that was one of my favorites in Zimbabwe. Like many large, densely-populated U.S. cities, once you get a parking spot next to your residence, you don't want to give up that spot. That's why we left the car at home and did finally take public transit, which was my first of many times on Chicago's Metro Transit System as we used both the train and bus. One of the fun things I enjoy is people watching and being on the trains and buses was a fun experience. The dinner was amazing and eating at Nandos brought back fond memories of Zimbabwe.

After we got home from dinner and my niece went to bed, I had a rare opportunity to speak candidly with my cousin about her life—the first time we had an adult conversation. We sat, talked, and bonded until 1 AM. Although we have a ten-year age difference, spending time with her renewed the respect my husband and I have always had for her. She is an independent woman who has made a way for herself in the United States after arriving as a teenager in 2000, not long after us. She stepped up to support her younger sister when she became a single mother and she does a great job of co-parenting my niece. I am grateful I got the time alone with her and reconnected before my other cousin arrived from Ohio.

Friday was our day to explore downtown Chicago where we had an incredible time. We rode the bus to downtown. The weather was clear so we had gorgeous views of the city skyline and Lake Michigan. We rode past Loyola University, walked to the famous Millenium Park, the Art Institute of Chicago, the renowned Garrett Popcorn store, the Civic Opera Building, and stopped for a snack at Food Truck Friday by the Richard J. Dailey Center. The bacon, date, and goat cheese empanadas were delicious. By end of the day, we had taken in the planetarium and had seen most of the landmarks. According to my step tracker, that Friday I walked a little less than nine miles.

Dinner on Friday night was also a first for me. My hosts took me to Ras Dashen Ethiopian Restaurant. I was excited to try something new because I do not usually deviate from what I like to eat, but both my cousin and niece were excited to take me to their favorite Ethiopian place. The food was amazingly delicious. My cousin is a vegetarian and my niece and I ordered lamb that was exquisitely seasoned. At the end of dinner, my cousin bought me Ethiopian coffee beans that tasted so good (I am a huge coffee fan). We got the bus home again and I was beginning to understand and enjoy this public-transit life.

My cousin from Ohio arrived later Friday night and it was a treat seeing her. My cousins and I text each other at least once a week but seeing them in person after a couple of years was exciting. This cousin is a single mother of a rambunctious, opinionated, and intelligent, nine-year-old girl and she has successfully faced the challenges of raising a child. Thankfully, her sister in Chicago has been a tremendous support and she loves the child as her own. We stayed up talking until 3 AM Saturday morning and although we were all tired when we got up a few hours later, we were out the door at 9:30 AM, heading out to explore the Chicago Navy Pier. I was excited to ride the Navy Pier Wheel and photograph the picturesque skyline. That was another first for me.

Prior to my trip, my niece had requested that I bring a swimsuit because she wanted to go swimming with me. After our visit to the Pier, we drove to Kenosha, Wisconsin to visit their weekly outdoor farmers and craft market, to sightsee, and then to go swimming. We rode a trolley that took us around the small town and were able to see downtown Kenosha before we found a secluded beach. Even though the water was freezing, I swam with my niece and had an incredible time. Swimming on a secluded beach and having a picnic on the shores of Lake Michigan were other firsts for me.

What I enjoyed most about this trip, apart from traveling alone, was exploring the tourist attractions and learning about the city. When our family goes on vacation, my husband and children do not enjoy doing the tourist-type activities. In most cases, I insist that we do and learn something new about the places we visit, so it was fulfilling to see what I wanted to see and experience new things for the first time. As a mother and wife, it is also liberating and rejuvenating not to have to be a caregiver, but just to have some fun. My weekend of firsts was a whirlwind and I was exhausted, but it was worth it.

Why do I include this in my book on losing myself? It shows just how "lost" I was that a simple weekend visit to Chicago could be so liberating. I had to overcome my fear and guilt of leaving my son behind. I had to face all the events and experiences like this one I had abandoned and forfeited because I got lost in the events of my life. I am learning to be proactive to help make some things happen, for if I wait for the right things to occur, they probably won't. One area that I am still searching for answers of how to find myself is in the area of my career, and in the next chapter, I will relate some of my progress on that front as I continue to fight the war of finding myself and my purpose.

Chapter 13

Shocked By How Much I Knew

In late 2016, the university where my husband worked asked me if I would teach two classes that had never been offered before. It had been two years since I taught, and initially I was not interested. They kept asking, however, so eventually I agreed. I reluctantly shelved the excuses I had rehearsed many times and had developed a convincing list of excuses that sounded reasonable to me—but I only agreed to teach one of the classes.

These classes represented the first graduate course I would teach by myself. In the past, I had co-taught a research methods class with my husband. I enjoyed that experience, but in 2016, I felt detached from my professional aspirations. I had not seriously thought about what my next professional steps were because I felt boxed in by personal and family matters and didn't see any way I could pursue a career path. Before graduating with my doctorate, I had an idea of what I wanted to do in academia, but that seemed like a distant memory and remote possibility.

When I started my doctoral studies, I wanted to work at a reputable research university and take the publish-or-perish route to professional advancement and fulfillment. When I learned more about that work environment and observed how contentious and competitive it was when researchers navigated complex political relationships between professors, I decided against that course of action. When I graduated, I thought getting a job at a regional university would be a great fit and fulfilling for me. That possibility has not worked out and four years after graduating, I had applied to several universities with no favorable responses. One promising position fell through because the funding was denied for the program. I had no choice but to remain at home, mainly caring for our son.

I am glad I decided to teach the class on international issues and trends for it was one of the most fulfilling professional experiences I have had in a long time. The first night of class was the presidential inauguration night on January 20, 2017. I knew that the international policy changes President Trump had promised during the first 100 days of his administration would provide many opportunities to draw from real-life examples to enhance the content of this class.

On the first night I was not nervous, but instead found myself excited, well-prepared, and ready to do a good job of making the material interesting and applicable for each student. The class had four students, which is normal for graduate courses at this university. The students were from the United States, Malawi, the United Kingdom, and Brazil. That also excited me because it meant their different perspectives would enhance the learning for each student as they drew from one another's diverse backgrounds.

In every class I teach, I always start the evening with a devotion and prayer. For this class, I used material from a devotional from the psalms titled *Your Life Matters.* I had started reading it and found it instructional, encouraging, and challenging for me as a believer. At the beginning of every night, a devotion helped students refocus and put aside whatever challenges were affecting their learning experience. I then prayed for them and their families. Prayer also helps them focus and starts each evening smoothly. For the time we spent together in class, we could all focus on the subject matter and hopefully shut out "life." When I pray, I know the Holy Spirit helps me be an effective communicator.

I am a life-long learner. It is always in my best interest to know current events and what is happening around the world. I learn from watching the news and reading a cross-section of news sources, along with books and magazines. I have done this for so long that I take it for granted, not realizing how much more I know about the world compared to the average American. I attribute part of this interest in the world to my education in Zimbabwe.

Despite my value of being a lifelong learner and the time I invested in reading and watching, I was shocked at how much I knew about the world. Teaching that class was effortless and integrating the textbook material with real-life world examples was exciting and easy for me. I was enthusiastic about the class subject and my students picked up on it and they were excited too. After the first night of class, one of the students suggested we do a cultural food night so we could share a dish from each country represented in the class. It was fun for me as a professor to see the students immerse themselves in the course while having a genuine interest in each other's cultures.

During the course, I was confronted with the reality that my students did not know much know about the state of the world. During lectures, I would bring up examples I assumed the students were familiar with, things like the civil war and atrocities that occurred in Darfur, South Sudan. To my surprise, they had no idea what I was talking about. On more than one occasion, I had to pull up YouTube videos to demonstrate what I was referring to. My ability to educate the students and integrate faith and learning were important parts of my teaching philosophy. I challenged them as believers to care about what was happening in the world. It was exciting and fulfilling to draw from my experience working for The Voice of the Martyrs and integrate the various ways that ministry supports persecuted Christians in the many parts of the world covered by the textbook.

Throughout the class, the students gave me positive

feedback concerning their learning experience. I was encouraged when on the last night of class, one student thanked me for the course and told me she wished my class was the last one she had to take for her master's degree because that would have meant she would be finishing on a high note (she had one more class to take before she earned her degree).

Another student told me he enjoyed school but the only reason he was in graduate school was because it was the only way he could stay in the U.S. He added that since our class had started, he looked forward to coming to class and had enjoyed it. He also said he appreciated that I was from another country because I brought a unique perspective to the course. A third student said she enjoyed the class because she learned a lot she did not know and had been sharing her knowledge with her roommates. While I do not teach for accolades, it was a blessing to hear the impact the course and my teaching had on those students. The possibilities for my future are endless and I am on a journey to find out where each experience takes me as I find myself and fulfill my God-given purpose.

I was gratified that I was able to teach a graduate class by myself and not have my husband as a safety net. When I think back to when I started teaching college classes, I had confidence and did not have the need to rely on my husband. After a while, my confidence had plummeted and I had used my husband both personally and professionally as a shield and in some instances as an excuse to avoid doing things on my own. Having to care for our son and shouldering most of that responsibility became excuses not to do some things or avail myself of the available opportunities. Our son's behavioral challenges also reduced my number of interactions with others.

I now realize that since my graduation in 2012, I had stopped developing personally and professionally. Generally, I did not use my creativity or pursue my purpose. In hindsight, I understand why and how I ended up where I am. It was partly because I did not understand what my purpose is and so I had not developed my creativity. I was also not aware of the importance and responsibility I had to use my God-given gifts. I was being a poor steward of who He made me to be.

Teaching the course gave me an opportunity to delve into and re-explore possibilities about my professional future. Even though I decided to teach the class in 2016, my meeting-turned-coaching session with my life and purpose coach prepared me to embrace the opportunity. From that eye-opening interaction, I was open to see how this teaching experience was an integral part of my self-rediscovery of purpose and creativity. Right now, I don't know what this positive teaching experience means in the big picture of my professional future, but I am okay with that. I am a work in progress.

As my coach reminds me often, figuring out one's purpose and embracing creativity are not a destination, but a journey. Based on my DISC personality profile, I am a "peacemaker." This means that among other characteristics, I am careful, I think things through, I am slow to make changes, I am predictable, and my ideal environment is stability, predictability, as well as tasks that can be completed at one time. Being spontaneous, creative, and pushing myself out of my comfort zone, while also allowing myself to seek the Lord about my purpose and how He can use those creative gifts He has given me, are not my strengths. It has taken me time to re-focus my thinking and actively seek the Lord about what it all means, and it won't happen quickly.

Taking action steps to alter my thinking and allowing the process and journey to develop organically are challenging, but I am slowly learning to be more intentional, while not reverting to old patterns of comfort. I have embraced my coach's prescription of doing something fun and creative for myself every week and trying new things while pursuing and embracing new opportunities. I am a smart, intelligent woman who has extensive experience in a variety of fields, and I continue on the journey to discover my purpose and use my creative gifts to impact the lives of others. The journey of self-discovery continues as you will read in the next chapter.

Chapter 14

Off to Dallas

In 2017, I went on another solo trip to Dallas, Texas for the National Conference on Race and Ethnicity in Higher Education. I chose that one because I enjoy discussing and studying social justice. It was put together by the University of Oklahoma, my alma mater, specifically by the Department of Human Relations. I earned my master's degree in human relations, and I did part of my coursework for my doctorate in human relations, social work, and education.

Not only was I interested in the subject matter, but it was clearly another chance to get away from home and the first time I had ventured out on my own as a professional since I graduated in 2012 (Chicago was a personal trip). It represented the first opportunity not to be enmeshed in my husband's identity personally or on the job. It had been a while since I had done something for myself professionally, and we personally paid for the registration and my hotel stay. My husband was totally supportive of my going.

It was the first time in years I had gone somewhere where I didn't know a single person. It was scary but exhilarating at the same time. I was forced to step out of my comfort zone and go to a conference where no one was talking about special needs. There was a 100-page catalog of available seminars I could attend and talks I could listen to, and I alone decided which ones I wanted to participate in. It was exhilarating.

The drive to Dallas was amazing. I stopped at Starbucks along the way and the thought came to me that I was going to drive for three hours and not hear "Mom, can I? Honey, can you?" It would just be me, my podcasts, and my music, or I could just drive in silence and think.

I had another bout with guilt as the time approached to depart because part of the challenge of having a child with autism is that you must tell them ahead of time what's going to happen and talk them through it all. There can't be any surprises. The days leading up to the trip were filled with anxiety as I considered all the things that could go wrong. What's more, would I even be able to get away, or would something happen to prevent it?

Also, I questioned whether I should really be

spending our family's money on a week away. The registration alone was $900, and there was the cost of staying in an expensive hotel across the street from the conference, chosen because I could not walk very far, especially in the summer months, due to the nerve damage in my leg.

I also wanted to be close to the conference because they were screening social-justice documentaries in the evening and since I didn't know anyone and was by myself without any colleagues, I was planning ahead for my own safety. Driving, arriving, finding the parking garage, and then checking into the hotel were all a big deal. Then I got to take out all my jewelry and clothes and place them on the bed, which was also refreshing.

One thing I don't get to do with a special needs child is leave anything laying around, whether it's expensive perfume or something simple, because he might pick it up and decide to throw it or drop it in the trash. That means I could never leave jewelry lying around. Being able to lay out all my stuff in the hotel bathroom or my clothes for the week was a treat, as was deciding on the spur of the moment to take a walk.

The conference started on Monday and we got to attend a specific seminar for the first day. I decided to go to one taught by an administrator from a university in Michigan, a lawyer by profession and the university's diversity officer. Her seminar was on how to incorporate diversity in the classroom in a predominately white institution (PWI). It was fascinating. At the beginning of that session, we were asked to introduce ourselves. At our previous school, my title was Special Assistant to the President, so when they asked me what I did, I said Special Assistant to the President and had to divulge that I was the wife of a president of a PWI.

As soon as I introduced myself and had to bring in my husband into it, I thought *I'm not doing that again. I have to change how I identify myself because then if I say I am the wife of the president, I open myself up to having to talk about that part of my life.* I started referring to myself as Bongi with Southwestern University, an adjunct faculty member who was interested in social justice. This was an opportunity for me to extricate myself from my identify in terms of my husband so I could have my own identity. I thoroughly enjoyed it, and I saw it as an important step in defining and declaring who I am.

I can't remember what presentation I went to on Tuesday, but there were workshops and sessions every ninety minutes. I attended one session on social justice and one that I ended up getting into an argument with the presenter, which also helped me take a step closer to defining who I am. The presenter was talking about diversity in education and the use of the n-word (the American derogatory term for a person of color) in academic literature as it relates to diversity. He was an African-American and I was sitting next to black students from the University of North Dakota. He started talking about how he traveled across Asia and had come across the n-word being used in Asia to describe people of color.

When he cited where he had seen the use of the word, he wasn't giving us factual information in terms of specific places and areas. I had an issue with him basing his talk on what I deemed anecdotal instead of empirical evidence. In my opinion, he was dealing with something that was highly sensitive, yet he was talking down to a group of young people who were taking issue with his premise. He was agreeing with people like Al Sharpton that we should bury the word and not use it, but the young people thought differently. They felt they could "sanitize" the word and use it amongst themselves.

He mistakenly used the word that I grew up hearing, which is similar to the n-word, and that word is *kaffir*, which is what white colonialists used to describe black people in Africa, including Rhodesia before it became Zimbabwe after independence. I took great exception to his connection with that word. Finally, I raised my hand and challenged him, saying, "First, I have an issue with you giving anecdotal evidence without empirical proof of what you're saying. Second, I have an issue with you not having data to prove your point while you're berating these young students."

His response was, "How do you know?"

I said. "Excuse me, I'm actually not African-American. I'm an African woman from Zimbabwe, from the Ndebele tribe. My country only has a few more than 13,000,000 people. What you are talking about, I've lived it. That is why I can stand here and say that what you are saying is not correct. If you had empirical data to back up what you're saying, that would be different."

He hemmed and hawed and the students from North Dakota seated next to me backed me up, and everyone else around the room started to say the same. They were questioning him about the evidence on which he based his thesis that the n-word was being used everywhere. To prove his point, he picked out Asia and reasoned that we should stop using the n-word because now "everyone else" was using it.

I felt great challenging him, especially when I was walking out and the students were telling me I did a good job. I ran into several of them at Starbucks later that evening and they again told me what a good job I had done. They were thinking what I was saying, but they did not have the words or courage to say it. They said I told it exactly how they were thinking it. I walked out of there thinking, *Yes, I have found myself!*

I was not speaking up in that session because I was offended, but because I was confident in what I knew. I have read a lot about social justice, which is fascinating to me because I'm not an African-American, so I look at it through a different lens based on who I am and what I call my "lived experience" as a qualitative researcher. It's interesting when I look at things through my life experience, while also being exposed to the academic perspective where we must have facts to back up our arguments. We can't just have a pie-in-the-sky thesis and assume that because we are talking about a place that's outside of the United States, people are simply going to accept it.

My other highlight was attending a presentation on "Colorism." This was the high point of the whole conference for me and for many others, for the conference room had more people than chairs, and it was a large room. The premise of the presentation was that some people's behavior toward others is not only based on the color of the other person's skin, but the exact color and is best represented by what is called the brown paper bag test. During American slavery, the hue of a slave's skin determined whether or not he or she worked in the fields or in the house. The fairer someone was, the better jobs they got. The darker they were, the worse jobs they were assigned. It has become a whole field of study in higher education. Colorism still exists in the African-American community and culture in general.

When the session started, the presenters asked us

to pull our sleeve up, look at our arm, and write down the word we would use to describe our skin tone. We all got our notebooks and wrote down the word that described our skin color. (I wrote down the word caramel to describe mine.) When we were done, they asked us to group and gather ourselves around the room based on our self-identifying word, from the lightest to the darkest hue of skin. Even Caucasians were asked to group themselves based on skin tone. We lined up, starting with a group of white people and then having groups that ranged the whole way down the spectrum. This practice is known as self-identification.

I was standing with my skin color group next to a lady I had never met. She said to me, "You see that woman across the room?" She described where that woman stood in line from a certain point, so I counted down to see who she was referring to. I noticed that the woman kept looking over at us. Then the lady next to me reported, "That's my cousin. We don't talk. Her hair is curlier than mine. Her skin is lighter than mine, and because of that, we don't talk." I was hearing and seeing an example of colorism right next to me!

Then they told us to count one to seven, and then form a circle with the people from other groups who had our number, so we broke up into seven circles of people with representatives from each color group. We were then told to debrief about the exercise, sharing the word we used to self-identify and how it made us feel. I could already tell by their body language that some people who were of the darker skin tones were not very happy.

Then they brought us back together and asked a few people to share what they discussed in their group.

At that point, a white lady raised her hand and informed us that she was feeling quite emotional, and some of us rolled our eyes. She went on to say that she had never, ever considered herself as someone who thought she was better than anyone else. She told us how she was raised never to see color. To give us an example, when she was a little girl, her mom had taken her to the store in the small town where she lived. She really wanted a doll and it was a black doll. We all started looking at each other wondering what the point of her story was.

She informed us that she was raised in the South but finally her mother bought her the doll, which she loved very much. Then she was out in public when some black men hit the doll out of her hand and the doll fell into the water. She cried and cried for weeks for her black doll. She knew she could not be a racist because she cried so hard after she lost her doll.

Then I noticed a woman who looked like she was biracial, pacing in the back of the room. The more she paced, the angrier she was getting. Before this white woman finished her long story, this young lady interjected to say, "I feel triggered right now." I had never heard the word *triggered* used before. The room got very quiet and she went on a rant. She said, "Because your f-ing mom bought you a f-ing black doll, you think you can relate to my experience?"

The moderators were dumbfounded before one interjected to say, "Let's take a break," but that young woman kept pacing. Some of us older women quickly went and gathered around her, telling her she could not get worked up and talk the way she was talking because everyone quits listening when that happens. She had to be able to say what she wanted to say without expletives and not seeming overly angry. We knew she had reason to be angry but the way she communicated it caused people to tune her out; she had to say it properly.

She refused, and I responded, "Okay, let me take you outside and we will walk it off. Go calm down and compose yourself and then maybe when you come back in you can properly say what you want to say." An elderly black lady informed me that this young woman was very disrespectful and I should not coddle her. She advised me to tell her that no one was going to listen to her because she thought she was the only one who could verbalize the struggle against racism. Meanwhile, all the Caucasian people went to the white lady to console her. Some people sat down somewhere between the two ladies and said, "This is just crazy."

The young lady felt the white lady was minimizing her view on race because she was speaking from her experience as a member of a different race. She didn't think that was the place or the time for her to communicate what she was communicating. She felt that the white person invaded her space and took over her story. It is common today for people to talk about having their safe spaces. The white woman was talking nonsense that no one else could relate to except maybe a few other white people, and she had taken away the safe place for others.

We had to leave that seminar not having really resolved anything because it became about consoling the lady with the black doll and also calming the other young lady. That was fascinating for me. I had learned about colorism in graduate school but had never experienced anything like that where the discussion ended up being hyper-emotional, with everyone believing they were right because of how loud they were. In that scenario, people are not listening to one another, let alone learning from one another or their experiences.

One of the nights, I attended a movie about mascots in sports and how Native American symbols have been co-opted by sports teams. It was a documentary on how some of those mascots, like the Washington Redskins, had become a big issue in the NFL. Certain Native American tribes found it offensive that an NFL team would be named Redskins. They gave the historical context for that term. The Kansas City Chiefs was another team mentioned. Several universities and high schools had changed their mascots because of issues Native American tribes had with those symbols being used for profit or in a way they found wasn't uplifting. That was also fascinating for me as someone who came to this country as an adult.

On another night, I watched a film about the need for prison reform because of the discrepancies in sentencing guidelines for different crimes that impact people of color. This topic is called restorative justice, a term I had heard about. Watching a documentary on the benefits of restorative justice compared to punitive justice was intriguing. Being able to ask questions was wonderful. The moderator had distributed a rough draft of the documentary, and one of the questions she asked afterwards was if we thought there was anything she left out.

Of course, I raised my hand and said she left out for-profit prisons and what research has termed the school-to-prison pipeline. This is an important social justice issue I had been reading and learning about, which looks at the approach to education, social justice, human relations, and social work. The way we finance our schools in the U.S. is to tie our school budgets to property taxes.

For example, individuals in south Oklahoma City don't have as many resources as families in richer areas, so kids in their local public school get less educational resources when compared to those of the kids on the north side. That impacts not only the quality of teachers they have in the schools and the after-school programs, but it also impacts the type of discipline administered to students who have behavior problems.

For example, in Oklahoma City where we used to live, if we look at the disciplinary procedures and protocols for students in the school where my son went and compare them to those in Oklahoma City public schools, we learn that there is a different disciplinary system based on demographics. The system in the poorer districts tends to be stricter and more punitive. When we look at the U.S. as a whole, we realize that the proliferation of for-profit prisons has been linked to the school-to-prison pipeline.

Those prisons need residents, so stricter prison sentences among the poor is the same issue as the stricter discipline in poorer school districts. Justice is not being distributed evenly among the poor and the rich. Therefore, we are funding a system that unfairly treats brown and black individuals, especially males, which brings the focus to single-parent households here in the U.S. Brown and black single-parent households when compared to Caucasians and other races have a much greater representation among the prison populations nationwide.

This imbalance in sentencing policies occurs when punitive guidelines are put in place in schools instead of restorative processes, which then disproportionately affects children of color compared to their white counterparts. When we look at the research, the punitive justice within the schools compared to the restorative is actually mostly in inner-city schools. The private schools in high income areas will have more leniency because they may not be dealing with the systemic and social problems that lead to some of the disruptive behaviors.

Another thing I added to the discussion was that the facilitator didn't address how restorative justice comes into place when we are talking about youth that may have special needs. Because they live where they live, they don't have the family support or medical care access for diagnosis to properly deal with some of the underlying causes of behavior issues. She thought those were great comments, so it was another time when I felt I made a significant contribution. I didn't want that week to end, but it did.

I came back home refreshed, challenged, and feeling like I had learned a lot, not only about myself but about subjects I'm interested in. My experience and expertise came full circle when Reggies was interviewing for his latest position at Ottawa University in Kansas. One of the first things I noticed based on my interests was that this was one of the only institutions I knew that had a diversity statement. When it came to issues of social justice and diversity, I was coaching him for his interview. Having gone to Oral Roberts, Reggies hadn't had some of the experiential knowledge in that area, but he had read up on some of the issues they were going to ask him about at Ottawa. If they had asked me those questions, I would have answered them with no problem.

When we visited Ottawa and he interviewed with the faculty, I knew exactly what they were talking about when they asked him certain questions. I knew where they were coming from knowing that he had only worked in evangelical Christian higher education. I felt like I made a significant contribution.

As I write, we have been at Ottawa for one year, and I have already collaborated with the man who leads the diversity initiative at the school. We hosted a movie for students in the Black Student Union called *The Black Klansman*, a Spike Lee movie. We had a discussion afterwards about the themes in the movie to learn what the students thought about it.

Then we hosted, in conjunction with the city, a showing and discussion of the movie, *The Hate You Give*, which I've seen twice. We screened it for the city, our students, and the community to conclude Black History month and had a discussion at the end. I have taken the lead in opening the discussion by setting the ground rules. I pulled the themes from the movie, challenging the students' thinking so we could uncover and learn from their personal experiences.

One of the questions I asked in our discussion for *The Hate You Give* was how many of the students had "the talk" about policing tactics with Black citizens. All the black students raised their hands indicating they had "the talk" with someone close to them. For me, it was a revelation because until I got to America, I didn't know what "the talk" was. Until Trayvon Martin was tragically killed, people of color had that talk within their families, but not many white people knew what the talk was.

I am looking for more ways to get involved on the Ottawa campus and diversity is one way. To me, this is not a job because I enjoy what I am doing. I am going to the 2019 National Conference on Race and Ethnicity in Higher Education in Portland, Oregon, and I am taking with me the head of diversity at the university and the head of the faculty senate. I know it will open their minds to a lot of social-justice initiatives in universities around the country. They will also meet professionals who are doing work similar to theirs.

Since my intervention, I have made great strides in finding my voice and myself, coming out of my attitude that it was my job to take care of everyone—except myself. I am pleased with my progress, but there is always the reality of my situation that keeps me humble and doesn't allow me to make too much progress before it brings me back to the stark reality that my battle for identity and meaning is far from won, as I will explain the next chapter.

Chapter 15

Two Steps Forward, One Step Back

My professional progress was short-lived because in the summer of 2018, my husband's work stress in Oklahoma City came to an end when his contract was not renewed by the university. That meant a job search, but the Lord was gracious and my husband quickly found another position. It was not in Oklahoma, however, and that meant our family had to relocate to Kansas, from where I am writing this book. Any move is traumatic, but ours seemed to be even more so. If I would have heard my husband say what furniture would go where, or that the washer and dryer were better off in the basement, or heard my son ask me to take him on a drive, I was going to lose it.

As the long summer days dragged on slowly for me, our task of settling into our new house in a new state was progressing at a snail's pace. Although I was grateful for this new opportunity for our family and a new job my husband loves, I wondered why I was becoming more exhausted and overwhelmed while also in physical pain. I asked myself, *Who said I cannot be grateful for the blessings God gives me, but also not enjoy the process of obtaining those blessings?* In my case, the move to a new state was an answer to prayer, but the move was stressful and exhausting. It started with the stress, anxiety, and anticipation of not being able to close on our new house until three weeks *after* my husband started the job. Then it was trying to pack a whole house alone while caring for our son.

Deep down, I knew that transitions of any sort are taxing for me and yet even with this realization, it didn't make it any easier. As a wife and mother, when faced with transitions and change, I exert a lot of energy preparing for them, psyching myself up, while making plans for any potential, unpredicted eventualities. I attribute this to years of parenting a child with disabilities and the need to always be prepared. As a mother of a teenager on the autism spectrum, I have to approach transitions and change with as much positivity as I can muster. Even though sometimes as mothers we create unrealistic expectations for ourselves, the fact is that most people do not understand the challenges and energy it takes to live our daily lives, let alone move from one state to another.

As I sit here today, the expectations I set for myself are driven by the idea that as a wife and mother, I must handle and juggle all the things thrown my way. In reality, no one can handle everything all the time without support and help. As I have grown older and hopefully a little wiser, I realize that living like that causes me to try and control most aspects of my life, not asking for help or relinquishing some things to my husband, who is quite capable, while I neglect practicing self-care. All that results in exhaustion and is detrimental to both my physical and mental health.

Another challenge of our move was that the home we bought in Kansas was not on the market. Finding a home that met our needs in a small town was not easy, so our realtor approached a homeowner who travelled extensively and owned a home that we knew would be a great fit for our family. The only downside was when you buy a home that was not on the market, as beautiful as it is, no one could have prepared me for how dusty and in need of a thorough cleaning that home would be. Usually I prefer move-in-ready homes because with our son, it is difficult to undertake long-term, involved tasks due to his need for constant attention and supervision.

Therefore, along with the challenges of getting settled, I was also faced with cleaning the new house. Thankfully, our realtor recommended a sweet lady who has a cleaning business, and she cleaned all the kitchen cabinets while I unpacked it and stocked the pantry. With all that was yet to be done, we could at least eat.

When we were finally able to pack up our home and move overnight to Kansas, it felt like I had been on my feet for two weeks straight. By the way, throughout the move, my husband was working. To amplify the situation, our son, who also has challenges with transitions, was overwhelmed so I was always trying to proactively de-escalate behaviors when they occurred.

For example, when the movers arrived with our belongings, unloading the truck took longer than he expected. As a result, he impulsively and aggressively charged at one of the movers, so to stop the aggressive incident, I took the brunt of it. To decrease the possibility of any such incidents, I drove him around our city for three hours until the movers were done unloading. I internalized all the aggressive energy that came my way and my body was feeling sluggish and run down.

Another variable that made this move difficult was that I had been home with our son the whole summer, including the three weeks when my husband started the job and spent the weeks in Kansas. Caring for our son is tiring on a good day, but when I added hosting his teachers doing ESY with him in our home, packing, and a plethora of other events, I was overwhelmed. I could neither control nor have the human resources to delegate. My supply of grace was depleted.

Throughout the summer, I had a close friend with whom I texted back and forth many times a day. She has been a great source of encouragement and consistently has a verse, a lesson, or advice when I am struggling. Since I have spent so much time with our son, sometimes when I redirect his behavior, I know he is tired of me and doesn't hear me any longer. I have been intentional not to raise my voice when correcting him and his recent responses to me have been "cool it" or "it's ok." Parents of typical 16-year-olds have the luxury to check out once in a while and have them entertain themselves for a couple of hours, but in my case that is not an option.

All the above could not have prepared me for what happened during the satellite installation. As days progressed, our son's impatience and incidents of impulsive behavior were increasing. For an hour or two one afternoon, he started following the technician around and I could see an aggressive episode coming. To stop, deflect, and manage that behavior, I convinced him to sit with me and calm down for a little. During the move, he had also begun spitting on me when he stopped listening, so when I asked him to stop spitting, before I could see it coming, he slapped me across the face. For a moment, I sat and wondered, *What just happened?* I quickly walked into the master bedroom, slid against the wall, and cried as I called and texted my husband. Our son was apologizing by then, which is typical. He did something impulsively and immediately either regrets it or wonders, *What did I do?* My husband rushed home and took care of our son for the rest of the day so I could get some rest and regroup.

As I reached out to my friend to tell her what had happened and how I was feeling, unlike in the past when I have sanitized my experience and feelings, I told her exactly how I was feeling— overwhelmed, stressed, and sad—and asked for prayer. Later that evening, I texted her:

> What a day. I haven't had one of these in a couple of years. Thank you for being there for me. The blessing and curse of autism is once a (negative) behavior is over on their part, it's on to the next (thing). He just came and said "Sorry, please forgive me, Mommy."

Heartbreaking! Living with ASD aggression is one of the toughest things I've had to deal with. The sad reality is there is no end, except to continue to pray for healing and hopefully interventions.

It was a tough day, but I am grateful I had a friend I could reach out to and be encouraged and supported.

Recently she reminded me of the importance of us continuing to pray and embracing the fruit of the Spirit, including long-suffering, which we sometimes overlook. Although I have perfected the practice and skill of long-suffering, it is important to remember that no matter how hard it gets, God is still on the throne (see Galatians 5:22-23). Although I don't know what He has in store for our son, myself, or our family as it relates to autism, His word never lies. The same God who rose from the dead, the God who created our son, is still in charge and our job is to continue believing despite the spitting, slapping, or whatever else comes our way.

I don't want to end this book on a downer or negative note, so let me make some concluding comments in the next chapter that summarize my journey to date and what I have learned and what I am still learning.

Concluding Thoughts

In 2016, I enlisted the services of a life and purpose coach, something I highly recommend for everyone. During our first meeting, he asked me what my purpose was. I thought autism and disabilities was where my purpose was. That's what I had been living in for such a long time so I did much research and was familiar with the problems and lifestyle.

Then my coach asked a question that changed my life and perspective: *Why would you want to do something that's going to depress you all the time. Your purpose is something that gives you joy. Whatever purpose God puts in your life causes you to wake up wanting to do it. It's not a job. You just enjoy what God has placed before you.* I'm starting to see that reality actualized in my life.

God's purpose for my life is so much bigger than just autism and disability. I told my coach that I was passionate about diversity and social justice. He asked me what that meant. I had to go full circle for me to realize and accept that that was my purpose. I knew what my purpose was in my head but I was so involved in doing things in my life that I had lost the passion for it. Maybe the concept hadn't permeated my being the way it should have. I had not allowed God to identify for me what that looks like in my purpose.

His question confused and frustrated me and I thought he was indicating that social justice was not my passion. That confusion caused me to second-guess myself, but caused me to dig deeper and helped me uncover some important things. *Was this truly who I was or did I simply study human relations in graduate school because it was available or seemed like a good focus? Did I study some social justice and diversity issues because they were interesting or was it my purpose? Is this what I'm really passionate about and what you've called me to do as my life's work?*

In God's plan and purpose, God's timing is perfect. Many times we don't see that purpose. Reggies' new job in Ottawa arrived at the right time. I had worked through all those questions and challenges. I was able to coach him in regards to some of what he would be asked in the interview. I had become sure of myself, and it really benefited the family.

One principle that has played a big part in my progress is the truth found in Romans 12:1-2:

Therefore, I urge you, brothers and sisters, in view of God's mercy, to offer your bodies as a living sacrifice, holy and pleasing to God—this is your true and proper worship. Do not conform to the pattern of this world, but be transformed by the renewing of your mind. Then you will be able to test and approve what God's will is—his good, pleasing and perfect will.

I interpreted the process described in Romans as finding the right process, the steps to take, so that I could find my purpose. I thought it was just something I logically did. Then it became apparent to me as I was going through this process, and read that passage, however, that I prayed, "Okay, Lord, what would you teach me? Are you teaching me about something that I went through in the past, what I'm going through now, or what do you have for me in the future?"

Part of the renewing of my mind was God taking me back to how excited and passionate I was in my classes in grad school about social justice issues, diversity issues, and inclusion. Then God brought the coach into my life when I needed somebody who understood not only diversity and inclusion but also reconciliation. I had to be reconciled within myself to say, "Lord, I know your plan for my life is bigger than being a wife and mother. I know those are important, but there is something bigger for me than those two important roles." That was my purpose and my past and present were preparing me to express it.

I had head knowledge that God is bigger than whatever circumstances I was in, but I was not allowing Him to work in and through me to show me what the bigger purpose was for my life. That search and journey are not comfortable but challenging.

When I looked at our marriage and after having studied our two personality profiles, I realized just how different my husband and I are. Proverbs 3: 5-6 instructs that, "Trust in the Lord with all your heart and lean not on your own understanding, in all your ways submit to Him and he will make your paths straight." This verse encourages me to trust God with our marriage and our differences because He brought us together. As James 1:17 instructs, I have to hold on to the reassurance that God as our Father gives us good things, which includes my spouse, and that we can stay strong in our faith in each other. We can rely on His unchanging strength and power (see Ephesians 6:10).

I went through a phase where I was fearful to be honest and vulnerable when it came to some of the challenges we faced as a couple. When I realized how uneven the responsibilities were, however, I began trying to figure out how that would work out and look. My coach told me not to think that whenever I was being honest, vulnerable, and open that I was dishonoring my husband in any way. In marriage, we end up also thinking that if we are honest about how I feel he (or she) may think I am dishonoring him or I don't love her, which goes against what the Bible teaches in terms of honoring each other as husband and wife. If we are not honest, open, and vulnerable, then we are not being the best person we could be in the relationship. That impacts how we search and discover the purpose God has for our lives. For me, I thought Reggies, my family, and my purpose were the same, but now I realize they are certainly not.

If I am not open, honest, and vulnerable, I end up

being miserable, which is how I was when we were pastoring in Zimbabwe. His calling is to preach and teach. My calling is to sound the alarm on issues that God has called me to talk about. Reggies was not preaching social injustice, or diversity inclusion and equity. He was preaching about what God called him to do and I need to do the same thing, and it is beautiful in God's sight and my own. Yes, my name is Sibonginkosi and my journey to discover who I am is well under way. With that being said, I am confident that the best is yet to come.

About
Bongi Wenyika, PhD

Bongi Wenyika received her journalism diploma from the Harare Polytechnic College in Mass Media Communication (Print Journalism) in Zimbabwe. She worked with such media organizations as Reuters News Agency and non-profit organizations. As a journalist, she developed an interest in women's issues and reproductive justice, self-development, and HIV/AIDS. She later transitioned from journalism to the corporate public relations field.

In the year 2000, she and her family moved to the United States of America where she furthered her education at Oklahoma Wesleyan University, majoring in Business Management and matriculated with a Master of Human Relations and Doctor of Philosophy degrees from The University of Oklahoma. Dr. Wenyika is passionate about social justice issues including diversity, inclusion, equity, criminal justice reform, education and advocates for individuals with disabilities and the aging.

She has served as a Court Appointed Advocate in

Juvenile Court, Oklahoma County. In 2017, Governor Mary Fallin appointed her to serve a four-year term as a board member to the Oklahoma State Council on Aging. Currently, Dr. Wenyika currently resides in Ottawa, Kansas with her husband Reggies, their two children, Thembi and Kudzai and dog Brian. She serves on the boards of Ottawa Community Arts Council and COF Training Services (servicing people with intellectual and/or developmental disabilities in Coffey County, Osage County, and Franklin County, Kansas).

You can contact Bongi Wenyika at:
bwenyika@gmail.com

WITHDRAWN

Made in the USA
Coppell, TX
17 November 2021

JAN 2 2